Cuirassiers and Heavy Cavalry

Dress Uniforms of the German Imperial Cavalry 1900=1914

D. S. V. Fosten

ALMARK PUBLISHING CO. LTD., LONDON

First Published—June 1973

ISBN 0 85524 130 6 (hard cover edition)
ISBN 0 85524 131 4 (paper covered edition)

FRONT COVER: Kettledrummer of Kürassier Regiment No 6 in Parade Dress.
BACK COVER: Kaiser Wilhelm II in the uniform of the Leib-Kürassier Regiment No 1. He wears the mantel with carmine piping on the cuffs, pockets and skirts. The collar is black velvet piped with white. Note the other officers in the unhang (Mansell collection).

Printed in Great Britain by
Vale Press Ltd., Mitcham, Surrey, CR4 4HR
for the publishers, Almark Publishing Co. Ltd.,
270 Burlington Road, New Malden,
Surrey KT3 4NL, England.

Acknowledgements

The writer wishes to thank David Nash and Laurence Milner of the Imperial War Museum for the invaluable assistance they gave in the preparation of this work. Thanks are also due to Ronald Harris for the generous help in allowing photographs from his very extensive collection to be used. R. Belmont-Maitland has also been very kind and allowed me to use photographs of some his extensive collection of helmets etc. The Mansell Collection and the Radio Times Hulton Picture Library have been useful in finding other photographs and Terry Macdonald has been extremely kind in printing some of the photographs. Wallis and Wallis have also been generous in allowing me to use photographs from their catalogues.

My especial gratitude to Robert Marrion and Douglas Hagger for producing the beautiful colour plates which help so much to complete this work.

D. S. V. Fosten,
Purley, Surrey, 1973.

BELOW: HM King George V of Great Britain (right) in the uniform of Colonel-in-Chief of the Kürassier—Regiment Graf Gessler (Rheinisches) No 8. At left is Tsar Nikolaus II in the gala dress of 1st Westphalian Hussar Regiment. (Mansell Collection).

Introduction

THE final step in the Bismarkian dream of the unification of Germany and the creation of the First Reich followed the Franco-Prussian War of 1870-1871. The King of Prussia, the most warlike and politically advanced ruler of the larger kingdoms, became the first 'Kaiser' and the new 'Germany' was given a modern federal constitution which it retained, even after the disappearance of William II, until finally dissolved by the revolution of 1918.

William I died in 1888 and the old 'Iron Chancellor' Bismark resigned in 1890. Thereafter the fate of the German nation became increasingly the responsibility of the 'Kaiser' who took an ever increasing share in the government of his country.

As far as the armies of the various kingdoms and dukedoms were concerned the federal constitution worked as follows:

(1) Contingents from the various States or Provinces became integral with the Prussian Army and wore its uniform.

(2) The troops of the Grand Duchies of Mecklenburg and Hesse became self standing contingents within the framework of the Prussian Army keeping certain uniform characteristics.

(3) The Royal Armies of Saxony and Württemburg retained their own War Ministries and Headquarter Staffs and Establishments and were bracketed in the 1st and 2nd Royal Saxon Army Corps (XII and XIX of the National Army) and the Royal Württemburg Army Corps (XIII of the National Army). These armies kept many characteristics of their old uniforms.

(4) The Royal Bavarian Army remained completely autonomous under the command of its King and with its own Headquarter Staff and HQ Establishments. It was formed in the I, II and III Bavarian Army Corps and retained its old uniforms bringing in some characteristics of the Prussian uniform and adapting them to their own needs.

The States and Free and Hanseatic Cities involved under (1) included Sächsen-Weimar, Sächsen-Altenburg, Sächsen Coburg-Gotha, Sächsen Meiningen, Schwarzburg-Rudolstadt, Schwarzburg-Sonderhausen, Anhalt, Lippe, Reuss, Schaumburg-Lippe, Bremen, Lübeck, Hamburg, Oldenburg, Waldeck-Pyrmont, Baden and Braunschweig together with Alsace Lorraine although the latter did not have the same standing as the remainder.

The differences in the uniforms of the various States were displayed on the helmet or shako plates, in the 'landeskokarden' which appeared together with the red, white and black 'reichskokarde' on the helmets and undress caps, in the sword knots, sashes, undress waist belts and the NCO's collar buttons.

ABOVE: Kaiser Wilhelm II in the uniform of the Garde du Corps with special black parade cuirass. (Mansell Collection).

The full dress uniforms were worn, with very little change, on all occasions up to 1907 when, for the first time, an official grey-green field service uniform was introduced.

The full dress uniform continued to be worn for parades, garrison guard mounting, church parades, walking out, social occasions, at court and at courts martial up to the outbreak of war. As late as 1910 the cavalry were wearing the full dress uniform at the Kaiser's Grand manœuvres.

Formation and Establishment*

The German cavalry was formed in Brigades, two Brigades to each Division, two Divisions to each Army Corps. The Prussian Guard Cavalry were formed into a Guard Division comprised of four Cavalry Brigades. The Army Corps comprised the Guard Corps, eighteen Prussian Corps, two Saxon Corps and a Württemberg Corps together with three Bavarian Army Corps. The Cavalry was controlled by an Inspectorate under the Command of an Inspector General. There were four Prussian Inspections numbered one to four with headquarters at Posen, Stettin, Strasbourg and Saarbrücken. There was one parallel Saxon Inspection with headquarters at Dresden and a Bavarian Inspection based at Munich.

According to a War Office source the total cavalry strength in 1912 approximated 2,600 officers, 225 Medical Officers, 330 Veterinary Officers, 215 Regimental Surgeons, 215 Paymasters and Assistant Paymasters, 105 Bandmasters, 205 Artificers, 10,330 NCO's, 60,500 rank and file and 69,900 horses.**

A regiment normally had five squadrons one of which was known as the 'Ersatzeskadron' and which acted as the Depot Holding Squadron. Each squadron comprised four troops (züge), each troop had four files (gruppe). The average strength of a squadron ranged from 4-5 officers, 136-142 NCO's and troopers and 146-150 horses (according to whether the regiment had a 'high' or 'low' establishment.***

The 'Gardes du Corps' had a separate establishment, given by the War Office source as 725 officers and men.

Schools, Inspectors and Academies

Prussia

General-Inspection/der Kavallerie—	4 Kavallerie Inspektion—Berlin
Unteroffizier/Vorschulen—	Annaberg, Bartenstein, Greifenberg, Jülich Sigmaringen (Neubreisach), Weilberg, Wohlau
Kavallerie—Kommissiarat—	Hanover
Militär-Reitschule/Inst.	Hanover
Offiziere-Reitschule—	Paderborn, Soltau
Kavallerie Telegraf-schule—	Spandau
Kriegsakademie—	Berlin
Milit. Vet. Inspektion—	Berlin

---

* Handbook of the German Army 1912—War Office Publication
** The regimental history of the 6th Kürassier Regiment, gives a breakdown of the unit at the outbreak of war; briefly this gives 104 officers, 20 trumpeters, 895 troopers together with 52 ancillary offices such as Veterinary Surgeons and Medical Officers. The regimental staff of the Saxon Karabinier Regiment comprised the Regimental Commander, a Staff Major, Adjutant, Ordnance Officer, Remount Officer, Baggage Master, Regimental Surgeon, Paymaster, Master Armourer, Trumpet Major and the Regimental Sergeant Major. A list of non commissioned ranks of the 6th Regiment gives: Etatsmässige Wachtmeister, Vize Wachtmeister, Sergeant—Trompeter, Sergeant, Unteroffizier, Sanitäts Unteroffizier, Zahlmeister and Unterzahlmeister.

The troopers of cuirassier regiments were titled 'kürassier', Gardes du Corps, 'gardist', Bavarians 'reiter', 1st Saxon Regiment 'reiter', the Saxon 2nd Regiment 'karabinier'.

*** According to the Handbook there were 69 effective squadrons in 1912 having what was known as the 'higher' establishment and of these 60 squadrons were Prussian, and 9 Bavarian. There were 441 squadrons having a 'lower' establishment, 335 of these were Prussian, 40 Bavarian, 40 Saxon and 20 Württemberger (25th and 26th Dragoons, 19th and 20th Lancers).

ABOVE: Kürassiers of Regiment Graf Gessler (Rheinisches) No 8 wearing the Koller (Full Dress Tunic) and carrying the standard lance. The standard bearer at right, next to the officer carries the standard in its protective oilskin cover.

Milit. Vet. Akademie—	Berlin
Milit. Lehr. Schmied—	Berlin
Remonte Inspektion—	Berlin
Pferde-Vorm. Kommissare—	Berlin
Armee Musik-Inspektion—	Berlin
Saxony	
Milit. Reitanstalt—	Dresden
Unteroffizierschule—	Marianberg
Remontdepots	
Pferdevormusterungs-Kommissare	
Hochschule der Schmiede	
Württemberg	
Kriegsministerium—	Stuttgart
Generalstab—	Stuttgart
Truppen-übungsplatz—	Munsingen
Bavaria	
Kriegsministerium—	München
Generalstab—	München
Inspektion der Kavallerie—	München
Militär Reitschule—	München
Kriegs Akademie—	München
Militär Schiesschule—	München
Unteroffizierschule—	München
Remonte Inspektion—	München
Militär Lehrschmiede—	München
Bekleidungsamter—	München and Wurzburg

CONTENTS

1: Prussian Kürassier Regiments and Gardes du Corps

THE Kürassiers were the senior cavalry arm of the old German Army. Their uniform was traditionally the yellow-white kirsey, with cuirasses from 1843. Before 1806 there were thirteen cuirassier regiments twelve of which were dressed in the yellow-white coats. The remaining one, the 2nd von Beeren Regiment had a lemon yellow coat.

After the Prussian military debacle of 1806 only four regiments can be said to have survived in regimental form, these were the Silesian No 1, the East Prussian No 2, the Brandenburg No 3, and the Gardes du Corps. These last being taken out of the numbered list in 1815.

In March 1819 four Dragoon Regiments became cuirassiers which resulted in the following organisation:

Regiment	New Title
Gardes du Corps	Gardes du Corps
Kürassier Regt No 1	1st Regiment
Dragoner Regt 'Königin'	2nd Regiment ('Königin')
Kürassier Regt No 2	3rd Regiment
Dragoner Regt No 2	4th Regiment
Dragoner Regt No 4	5th Regiment
Kürassier Regt No 3	6th Regiment
Kürassier Regt No 4	7th Regiment
Kürassier Regt No 8	8th Regiment

The Gardes du Corps continued to retain all the characteristics of the cuirassier regiments even though they had been removed from the numbered list. They had red facings and white buttons while the 1808 list gives the other three regiments black, light blue and red facings respectively with yellow, white and yellow buttons in that order.

In 1810 the Brandenburg Regiment were awarded blue facings later confirmed as 'cornflower blue'.

A table for 1819 gives the following facings for the eight regiments:

Regiment	Facings	Buttons
1st	Black	Yellow
2nd	Crimson	White
3rd	Light Blue	White
4th	Orange	White
5th	Rose Red	Yellow
6th	Dark Blue	Yellow

ABOVE: Officer giving orders to NCO's of Kürassier Regiment No 8 on a field exercise. Some of them have protective covers over their helmets and the two right hand men carry map and binocular cases. Man at extreme left has the 'M83' pattern pistol in its holster on the right side of his belt.

Regiment	Facings	Buttons
7th	Lemon Yellow	White
8th	Light Green with white piping on the collar and cuffs	Yellow

In 1821 the former Garde Ulanen Regiment was re-titled the Garde Kürassier Regiment and was given cornflower blue facings with white guard lace loops on the collar and cuffs.

The cuirassier uniform which comprised a black leather helmet with a high Romanesque crest of black horsehair, a short tailed double breasted coatee known as a 'kollet' and cuirasses was worn until 1842/3 when the steel or tombak helmet and the tunic ('koller') was taken into use. This latter costume continued to be worn with modifications until 1914.

Title	Raised	Garrison	Corps
Gardes du Corps	1740	Potsdam	Garde
Garde Kürassier Regiment	1815	Berlin	Garde
Leib-Kürassier Regiment Grosser Kurfürst (Schlesisches) No 1	1674	Breslau	VI
Kürassier-Regiment Königin (Pommersches) No 2	1717	Pasewalk	II
Kürassier-Regiment Graf Wrangel (Ostpreussishes) No 3	1717	Königsberg	I
Kürassier-Regiment von Driesen (Westfalisches) No 4	1717	Munster	VII
Kürassier-Regiment Herzog Friedrich Eugen von Württemberg (Westpreussisches) No 5	1717	1, 4, 5 squadrons Riesenberg 2 squadron Rosenberg 3 squadron Deutsch-Eylau	XX
Kürassier-Regiment Kaiser Nikolaus I von Russland (Brandenburgisches) No 6	1691	Brandenberg	III

Title	Raised	Garrison	Corps
Kürassier-Regiment von Seydlitz (Magdeburgisches) No 7	1815	Staff 2, 3, 4, 5 squadrons Halberstadt 1st squadron Quedlinberg	IV
Kürassier-Regiment Graf Gessler (Rheinisches) No 8	1815	Köln-Deutz	VIII

FACINGS AND BUTTON COLOURS

Regiment	Facings	Buttons
Gardes du Corps	Poppy Red	White
Garde-Kürassier Regt	Cornflower Blue	White
Kürassier-Regiment No 1	Black	Yellow
Kürassier-Regiment No 2	Crimson Red*	White
Kürassier-Regiment No 3	Light Blue	White
Kürassier-Regiment No 4	Red	White
Kürassier-Regiment No 5	Rose Red	Yellow
Kürassier-Regiment No 6	Russian Blue	Yellow
Kürassier-Regiment No 7	Lemon Yellow	White
Kürassier-Regiment No 8	Light Green	Yellow

* The officers' facing cloth was a good deal lighter than the crimson cloth used for NCOs and troopers.

Colonels in Chief (1913)

'Gardes du Corps'	His Majesty the Kaiser
'Garde Kürassier Regiment'	—
'Leib-Kürassier Regiment' No 1	—
Regiment No 2	Her Majesty The Kaiserin
Regiment No 3	Archduke Eugen Ferdinand of Austria
Regiment No 4	King Viktor Emanuel of Italy
Regiment No 5	King Wilhelm II of Württemberg
Regiment No 6	Tsar Nicholas II of Russia
Regiment No 7	—
Regiment No 8	King George V of Great Britain

RANK DISTINCTIONS

Cuirassier officers wore two different patterns of shoulder ornament. For full dress and ceremonials this was the epaulette and for the other duties the shoulder cords. The epaulette comprised a shoulder board in the colour of the full dress tunic edged with silver, black striped lace and with a large metal half moon or crescent in the button colour. The epaulette was retained on the shoulder by a small laced bridle (through which the epaulette passed), stitched on the shoulder of the coat and by a button at the collar end. The whole ornament was lined with cloth in the regimental facing colour. The rank was indicated by a system of stars and for the senior ranks also by fringing of bullion or metal wire in the button colour. The shoulder cord also had an underlay of the facing colour and a small frog which slipped under the shoulder bridle, at the other end they were also retained by a button. Ranks were indicated by (a) twisted silver and gold cords for the General Officers Range (b) twisted silver cords for the Field Officers and (c) straight silver cords for the Rittmeisters and Subalterns. In all cases the silver cords were mixed with silk 'darts' in the province colour.

Officers epaulettes

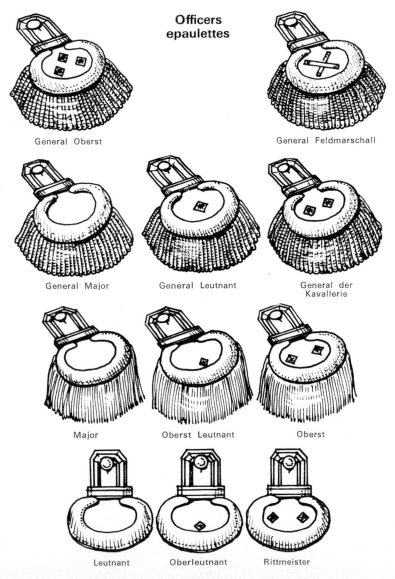

General Oberst   General Feldmarschall

General Major   General Leutnant   General der Kavallerie

Major   Oberst Leutnant   Oberst

Leutnant   Oberleutnant   Rittmeister

Rank	Epaulette fringe	Stars
General Oberst*	Bullion	Three
General der Kavallerie	Bullion	Two
General Leutnant	Bullion	One
General Major	Bullion	No star
Oberst	Thin metal fringe	Two (one on either side of device if applicable**)
Oberstleutnant	Thin metal fringe	One (below device if applicable)
Major	Thin metal fringe	No star
Rittmeister	No fringe	Two stars one on either side of device if applicable
Oberleutnant	No fringe	One star (below device if applicable)
Leutnant	No fringe	No star

Officers' epaulette pattern

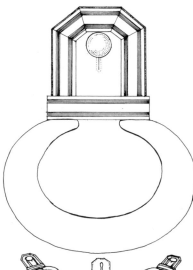

General Oberst with rank as Feldmarschall 1911-1914

Underside of an epaulette. The bridle was stitched to the coat.

General Oberst with rank of Feldmarschall before 1911

ABOVE: Officers' shoulder cords worn on an undress waffenrock on an undress occasion.

---

* General Feldmarschall had crossed marshalls batons, a General Oberst with the appointment of General Feldmarschall Four stars; until 1911 crossed batons plus three stars.

** The 1st, 2nd, 6th, and 8th Regiments carried the regimental devices on the epaulettes and shoulder cords.

General-Major	General Leutnant	General	General Oberst

Major	Oberst Leutnant	Oberst

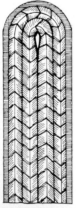
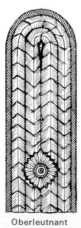

Leutnant	Oberleutnant	Rittmeister

RANK TABLE WITH ENGLISH EQUIVALENTS

Officers were split into three separate grades: (a) General Officers (b) Field Officers and (c) Captains and Subaltern grade.

Similarly the Non Commissioned Officers were split into (i) Senior NCOs entitled to wear the officers' swordknot (ii) NCOs without the officers' sword-knot.

German	English
(a) General-Oberst	No Equivalent
General de Kavallerie	General
General Leutnant	Lieutenant General
General Major	Major General
(b) Oberst	Colonel
Oberst-Leutnant	Lieutenant Colonel
Major	Major
(c) Rittmeister	Captain
Oberleutnant	Lieutenant
Leutnant	2nd Lieutenant
(i) The Etatmässige Wachtmeister	The Permanent Staff Regimental Sergeant Major known in the vernacular as the 'Spiess' had no equivalent
Feldwebel (Wachtmeister in cavalry)	Regimental Sergeant Major
Vizefeldwebel (Vizewachtmeister)	Squadron Sergeant Major
Offizier-Stellvertreter	No equivalent (acting officer)
Portepeefähnrich / Fahnenjunker	Ensign / Officer Cadet. No proper equivalent
(ii) Sergeant	Sergeant
Unteroffizier	Corporal
Gefreite	Lance Corporal
Einjährige-Freiwillige	One Year Volunteer
Kapitulant	Re-engaged Volunteer
Stabstrompeter (Had same rank as Feldwebel)	Trumpet Major
Trompeter (Had same rank as Unteroffizier)	Trumpeter

NCO's rank	Dress
Offizier Stellvertreter (Note: This rank was only brought in as as a wartime expedient and had no direct relevance to the uniforms described).	Gold or silver lace in the collar and cuff tunic braid with a large heraldic button* on each side of the collar. Cockades, sabre and sword knot of the officers' pattern. Rank and file shoulder straps but with an edging of gold or silver collar/cuff lace and appropriate regimental devices in officers' pattern.
Wachtmeister (Etatsmässige)	Gold or silver lace in the collar and cuff tunic braid with a large heraldic button on each side of the collar. In addition the Etätsmassige had a 1·6 cm strip of similar gold or silver lace around each arm 7 mm above the cuffs. Two strips of white, black striped, worsted braid on each overcoat collar patch. Officers' sword knot.

NCO's rank	Dress
Vizewachtmeister	Gold or silver lace in the collar and cuff tunic braid. Large heraldic button* on each side of the collar. One stripe of white, black striped, worsted braid on the overcoat collar patches. Officers' sword knot.
Portepeefähnrich	Ranked senior to the longest serving Sergeant. After passing the prescribed examination the 'fähnrich' became a degenfähnrich' and then ranked senior to the 'Wachtmeister'. Initially the 'fähnrich' wore the 'unteroffizier' distinctions with the officers' sword knot on the sabre. As a 'degenfähnrich' he wore the officers' sword and mutze and officers' cockades on the helmet. From 1910 a special overcoat was introduced for this rank. It had a single row of buttons down the front, the collar patches were decorated as for the Vizewachtmeister, the shoulder straps as the rank and file, and the back cut like an officer's paletot but minus the three buttons on each vertical pocket.
Sergeant	Gold or silver lace laid on the collar and cuff tunic braid plus a large heraldic button* on either side of the collar. Special NCOs sword knot. One stripe of white, black striped braid on overcoat collar patch.
Unteroffizier	Gold or silver lace in the collar and cuff tunic braid. Special NCOs sword knot. One stripe of white, black striped braid on overcoat collar patch.
Gefreite	A *small* heraldic button* on each side of the collar. The 'Gefreite' was the lowest ranking non-commissioned officer and was normally in charge of the barrack room, but mounted guard with the troopers. The 'Gefreite' could be appointed by the Commanding Officer of the regiment after he had completed six months service.
Trumpeter**	Normally ranked as 'unteroffizier' but could rise to the rank of 'Sergeant' or 'Wachtmeister'. In addition to their NCOs badges and the special trumpeter lace on collar and cuffs they wore 'schwalbenesten' (wings) of the regimental facing colour trimmed with similar gold or silver lace. The trumpet cords were of special design according to the province.

---

* These flat collar buttons were gold or silver according to the button colour of the regiment and were decorated with the heraldic device of the province ie, the eagle in the Prussian case.

** The 'trumpeter' as a title is a misnomer, in fact they were musicians capable of playing most of the wind instruments used by the military bands of the period.

Auszeichungsknopfe (The NCO's collar buttons)

Prussia

The Prussian heraldic eagle with the orb in the left claw and the sceptre in its right and with 'FR' on the breast.

Saxony

The Royal Arms of Saxony with crown, oval shield and lion supporters (heads looking back over their shoulders).

Bavaria

The Bavarian rampant lion, crowned and facing to its right.

| Prussian Kürassier | Saxon Reiter | Bavarian Schwere Reiter |

SCHMIEDE (FARRIERS)

The farrier ('Beschlagschmied') wore the regimental uniform with a small cloth horseshoe in the facing colour above the left cuff of the 'kollar' or 'waffenrock'. The Corporal Farrier ('Fehnenschmied') wore a similar badge but in gold or silver lace according to the button colour and the Sergeant Farrier ('Oberbeschlagschmied') wore the same badge but with a larger gold or silver horseshoe enclosing the smaller one. The NCO's wore the other distinctions of their rank where appropriate.

Beschlagschmied
Horseshoe badge in cloth material and facing colour of regiment

Falnenschmied
Horseshoe in gold or silver according to button colour

Oberbeschlagschmied
Two horseshoes in gold or silver according to button colour

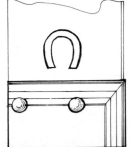
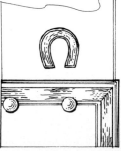
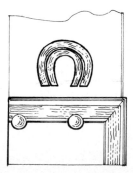

REGIMENTAL ADJUTANTS

The distinction of the adjutant was a woven silver thread sash worn over the right shoulder and slipped through a bridle on the left hip. The sash had a stripe in the province colour along either edge and two long tassels which descended to just above the knee. The sash was worn over the cuirass. The pouch belt was not worn by the adjutant. The Adjutants to Royal Princes wore, in addition, a silver aiguilette on the right shoulder.

When worn with the epaulette the sash was passed under the crescent part and outside the retaining bridle. When worn with the shoulder cords the sash was passed under the corded strap but over the frog.

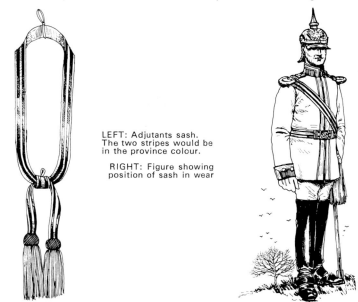

LEFT: Adjutants sash. The two stripes would be in the province colour.

RIGHT: Figure showing position of sash in wear

REGIMENTAL CHEFS AND GENERALS À LA SUITE

Colonels and Chefs of Kürassier Regiments with rank in the General Officer range wore the uniform of the regiment concerned but with the 'Generaladler' helmet plate. This was a crowned eagle looking to its right with horizontal outstretched wings and with the sword and sceptre in its talons. On its breast the eagle had the Silver Star of the Order of the Black Eagle with enamelled centre. The eagle was gilt for steel helmets and silvered for the 6th Regiment. An Army Order of July 31, 1860 stated that Generals were to be distinguished by the addition of feather plumes to the helmet in the province colours. A further Order of May 31, 1877 stated that they were not to wear the pouchbelt or the cuirass.

Generals à la suite (Supernumary Generals) wore the same uniform with Generals epaulettes etc, but with their rank indicated on the strap part. It follows that if a General à la suite was not in fact a General Officer he nevertheless wore a Generals full uniform but retained his own rank insignia on the shoulder cords or epaulettes. The Generals shoulder cords were entwined silver and gold cord, the central section round silver cord 'flecked' with silk darts in the provincial colour (black in the case of Prussia). The outer gold cord was flat.

Horse furniture was the regimental pattern as worn by officers and the Generals' paletots had carmine red piping and linings to the breasts.

RESERVE OFFICERS

Officers on the reserve wore the full uniform of their regiment when called to the colours. Their Reserve status was indicated by the addition of the old style Landwehr Cross which appeared both on the helmet plate and on the undress cap.

In the case of regiments entitled to wear the Guard Star as the helmet plate it was modified by the omission of the interwoven circular band and the cross was placed on the star so that the base rested on the motto circlet between 'SUUM' and 'CUIQUE.'

When the cross appeared on the 'linenadler' plate it appeared below the FR on eagle's breast.

The cross was worn in the centre of the Provincial cockade on the undress cap.

The cross was silvered on gilt helmet plates and gilt on the silver types.

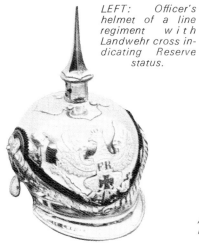

LEFT: Officer's helmet of a line regiment with Landwehr cross indicating Reserve status.

ABOVE: Trooper's helmet of a line regiment showing cross indicating reserve status.

STABSTROMPETER / MUSIKMEISTER
(TRUMPET MAJOR / BAND MASTER)

Special mention must be made of the uniform dress of this rank as it combined features of the dress of the officers, and the senior NCOs Before 1908 the trumpet corps and the military band were lead by a 'Stabstrompeter'. This man ranked as an NCO and had the same rank as the Etatsmässige Wachmeister' and wore the insignia of that status plus the traditional wings on the shoulders, and, in addition a long thin fringing to these ornaments in the button colour.

The Trumpet Major also wore special shoulder cords, interlaced after the senior officers fashion. If he were appointed to the rank of 'Musik-

ABOVE: Parade of a Line Kürassier Regiment. Note 'Stabstrompeter' in centre.

Trumpeters shoulder wing

Musikmeister collar lace
(Note high square cut collar)

Trumpet Majors
shoulder wing
and lace
(Pattern for Guard Regiment and Garde du Corps)

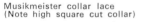

Musikmeister belt buckle pattern

Musikmeister shoulder wing

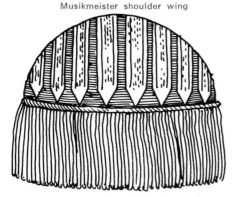

Musikmeisters
shoulder cord
in regimental
facing colour
with silver
lyre badge

19

Dirigent' usually a rank reserved for the 'higher establishment' regiments, he wore, in addition a narrow strip of braid along the centre of the shoulder straps.

If he were fortunate in being further promoted, to the exalted rank of 'Musik-Direktor' a further braid was added to the outside edge of the shoulder cords.

In 1908 the status of these NCO's was further enhanced by the creation of the rank of 'Musikmeister' in lieu of 'Stabstrompeter'. Although technically the rank was still non-commissioned it was considered superior to the 'Etatsmässige' and carried a quasi-officer pattern uniform.

The collar of the full dress tunic was higher and cut square in front instead of rounded so that it came right up under the chin. All the cuirassier tunic braid was in a mixture of silk and camel hair and the uniform was further enhanced by large twisted shoulder cords after the senior officer pattern but in poppy red cord except for the 5th Regiment where the colour was rose red, and the 2nd Regiment which had crimson cords. On the cords was a special silver lyre badge which was worn in addition to the regimental device (officers' pattern) where appropriate.

The undress cap, the frockcoat, the undress tunic, and the overcoat were in the officers' pattern with velvet facings where appropriate but with the special, cord shoulder straps. The greatcoat collar was grey when turned up and had no slit for the undress sword. The cloak was not permitted. A special pattern 'feldbinde' was worn. This was red leather, faced with cloth in the regimental facing colour with two stripes of silver NCO pattern lace edged on either side by a strip of black silk. The locket and clasp were in the button colour with a central ornament comprising the lyre. The pouch, bandolier and sword belt were in lacquered leather.

After five years in the rank of 'Musikmeister' the man could be promoted to the rank of 'Obermusikmeister' in which case a thin central gold cord thread was added to the shoulder cords.

The 'Musikmeister' continued to wear the wings with fringing but these were now decorated entirely in silver for both ranks and the lace bars were vertical instead of diagonal. The lace bars were point-ended and edged with a thread in the black Prussian province colour. Around the bottom of the wing was a thin silver cord from which the fringe was suspended.

The helmet was the NCO's pattern but with a taller spike. The cuirass was also the NCO's pattern.

On parade the trumpet was carried with silver and black cords and tassels.

EINJÄHRIG-FREIWILLIGE (ONE YEAR VOLUNTEER)

The one year volunteers were young men usually of solid, middle class background who, having attained an advanced standard of academic qualification were privileged to serve only one year instead of the obligatory three of their less fortunate comrades. The one year volunteer had a number of privileges, for example, he was permitted to choose his regiment and he was allowed to live out. He shared the service of a batman along with several other one year volunteers and usually messed with other volunteers in a restaurant. Generally they could rise to the

RIGHT: Einjährig—the Garde Küra-ssier—Regiment Freiwillige NCO's waffenrock of the Garde Kürassier Regiment showing twisted braid round the shoulder strap and figured braid in the tunic border on the collar and cuffs. (IWM).

rank of Sergeant and returned to serve their subsequent reserve service as Vizewachtmeister until they qualified for a commission. As Reserve Officers they usually rose to the rank of Rittmeister but were generally speaking, treated as inferior salt by the regular officer class. The distinguishing badge of the cuirassier one year volunteer was a twisted cord around the shoulder strap. The cord was in the province colour and had a two white and two coloured section, ie, two white twists, two black twists, two white twists and so on.

KAPITULANT (RE-ENGAGED PERSONNEL)

These were men who had served an obligatory length of service and had decided, of their own volition, to re-engage for a further period of service with the Colours. They were distinguished by the special sword knot (described under the separate section) and a strip of white worsted braid across the root of each shoulder strap where it joined the sleeve. The braid was decorated with a central woven stripe in the province colour.

STANDARTENTRÄGER (STANDARD BEARER)

The Standard Bearer was usually a Sergeant and was chosen from the best swordsmen in the regiment. The distinguishing badge was a shield worn on the upper right arm. The shield was in the colour of the tunic (white for Koller and dark blue for Waffenrock) and embroidered with two yellow flags with a crown above and the monogram WR II beneath. The cravats of these flags were white. The swordsmanship badges (chevrons) were worn under the shield. In addition the Standard Bearer wore a gorget suspended around the neck. The gorget was gold or silver according to the regimental button colour and was suspended by a chain. It was stamped with a design in the opposing metal, ie, silver on gold or gold on silver with two crossed flags, the 'WRII' cypher and two grenades. The Guard Regiment wore a gorget with the Guard Star and Royal Crown instead of the WRII cypher. Over the left shoulder the Standard Bearer wore a wide leather bandolier with two carbine hooks at the right hip. The bandolier was faced with regimental facing colour velvet and edged with the gold or silver lace according to the regiment. An edging of the facing colour showed along each edge.

ABOVE: Standartentrüger in Parade Dress showing well the standard bearers armshield and 2nd class Fechtabzeichen.

RIGHT: Standartenträger of the 8th Kürassier Regiment with the Standard and bandolier wrapped in their weatherproof black oilskin covers. Note also the standard bearers gorget worn high up next to the collar.

The bandolier of the Guard Regiment and the 1st, 4th, 7th, and 8th Regiments had gold or silver fringes down either edge according to the button colour. The end of the bandolier was decorated with a double 'carbine hook' which was used to fasten the bandolier to the metal bar on the haft of the standard.

Standartenträger of the 1st and 2nd Regiments wore their regimental gorgets above the special gorget of their appointment when they paraded without the cuirass. However, when the cuirass was worn with the gorget device on the breast part, the standard bearer's gorget was worn so that it came above it and both badges were visible.

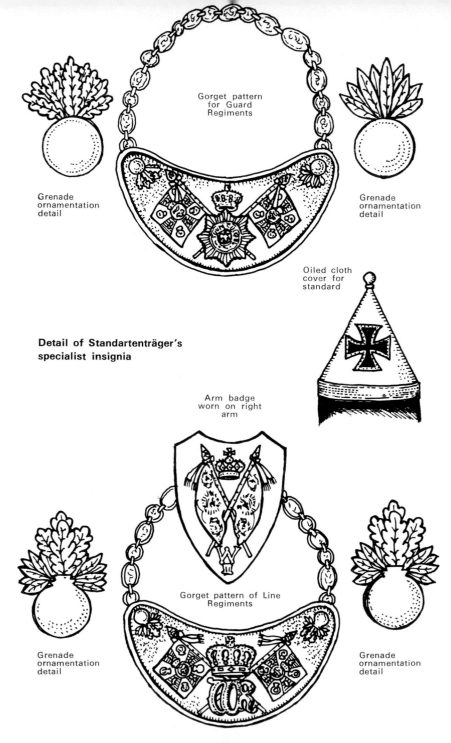

Gorget pattern
for Guard
Regiments

Grenade
ornamentation
detail

Grenade
ornamentation
detail

Oiled cloth
cover for
standard

**Detail of Standartenträger's
specialist insignia**

Arm badge
worn on right
arm

Grenade
ornamentation
detail

Gorget pattern of Line
Regiments

Grenade
ornamentation
detail

ABOVE: *Kürassier Regiment No 8 on leading man wears Fechtabzeichen 1st class on his right sleeve. All have the 'M98' pattern carbine in its bucket at the rear of the saddle.*

SPECIALIST BADGES

Fechtabzeichen (Distinctions of troops having achieved certain standards in fighting with the lance and sword)

These badges were authorised for the cavalry in 1889 and comprised a series of chevrons worn on the right upper arm. The Standard Bearers' shields and the signallers' badges were worn above them. The chevrons were as follows for the cuirassiers*:

1st Class —	1 woollen chevron in the facing colour
2nd Class —	2 woollen chevrons in the facing colour
3rd Class —	3 woollen chevrons in the facing colour
4th Class —	1 gold or silver lace chevron
5th Class —	1 gold or silver lace chevron and one woollen
6th Class —	1 gold or silver lace chevron and two woollen
7th Class —	1 gold or silver lace chevron and three woollen
8th Class —	2 gold or silver laced chevrons
9th Class —	2 gold or silver laced chevrons and one woollen
10th Class —	2 gold or silver laced chevrons and two woollen
11th Class —	2 gold or silver laced chevrons and three woollen
12th Class —	3 gold or silver laced chevrons

* These chevrons were also worn on the waffenrock.

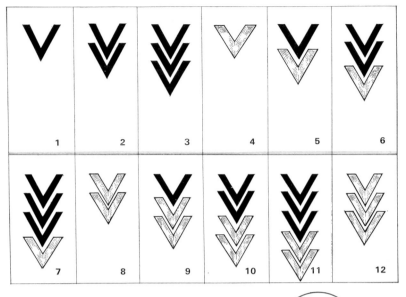

ABOVE: The twelve classes of Fechtabzeichen worn on the right upper arm of the koller and waffenrock. RIGHT: Flaggenwinkerabzeichen worn on the right upper arm above the Fechtabzeichen.

Flaggenwinkerabzeichen (Semaphore Badge of Signallers)

A circular piece of cloth of the colour of the tunic with two crossed flags with yellow staves. The rear flag white the front red.

Schützenabzeichen (Sharpshooter Badges)

From 1894 the cavalry took into use the infantry pattern sharpshooters badges. These comprised eight classes of plaited lanyards with rosettes and acorns and were worn on the left side of the koller and waffenrock from the shoulder strap to the second hook or button. The cord was a mixture of red, black and white woollen cord for the first three classes with the addition of one, two or three acorns. The 4th class had the lanyard only but in silver and silk cord and the 5th class the same plus a yellow metal crowned medallion. The 6th to 8th classes wore the same cord but with the addition of one, two or three acorns according to the class. The acorns appeared at the button end and the medallions at the shoulder.

Reitschulenabzeichen (Riding School Badge)

Personnel who had completed a one year course at the Military Riding Institute at Hanover wore a special twisted cord in the facing colour across the shoulder strap at the sleeve end. A two year course at the school was indicated by a double cord.

Militär-Telegraphenabzeichen (Telegraphist's Badge)

A strip of white, worsted braid striped in the province colour was worn along the pointed edge of the button end of the shoulder strap.

REGIMENT DER GARDES DU CORPS

The élite regiment of the Prussian cuirassiers, the Mounted Life Guards were raised in 1740, survived the 1806 catastrophe and thereafter enjoyed an uninterrupted regimental history until the end of World War 1. The regiment was garrisoned at Potsdam and was bracketed with the 'Garde Kürassier Regiment' in the 1st Guard Cavalry Brigade, the headquarters of which were in Berlin.

The 'Leib-Kompanie' had the added distinction of serving the Kaiser in a bodyguard capacity in the Royal Palace for which a special ceremonial uniform was worn.

Until 1888 the 'Gardes du Corps' had a ten company formation but were later re-organised in five squadron formation to conform with the other cuirassier regiments.

UNIFORM AND ACCOUTREMENTS

In general, the regiment wore cuirassier uniform with poppy red facings, white metal (silver for officers) buttons, 'Guard Lace' distinctions on the collar and cuffs of the tunics and the collar patches of the overcoats and an eagle crest on the helmet for parade and ceremonial occasions.

ORDERS OF DRESS

Garde du Corps Offiziere

Gala Anzug (Dress for Festive Occasions)
Helmet with parade eagle
Gala Waffenrock
Epaulettes
Gorget
Sash
Pouch and pouch bandolier
Short white gloves
Orders and Decorations
Riding Boots, jack boots and spurs
Sabre

Galawachanzug (Duty Dress for Palace Festive Occasions)
Helmet with parade eagle
Koller
Supraveste
Epaulettes
Sash
Gala pouch and pouch belt
Gala degentasche (sabretache)
Gauntlets
Riding breeches, jack boots and spurs
Sabre

Gesellschaftanzug (Dress for Social Occasions)
Helmet
Waffenrock
Epaulettes
Gorget
Short white gloves
Orders and decorations
Wide loose white linen trousers for summer or black/blue trousers for
  winter
Boots, with screwed on spurs
Sabre or Degen

Gardeanzug (Guard Dress)
Helmet with parade eagle
Koller
Epaulettes
Cuirass (special black cuirass if ordered)
Sash
Pouch and pouch bandolier
Gauntlet gloves
Orders and Decorations
Breeches and jackboots
Sabre
Paletot when guardsmen wear overcoat, mantel if mounted

Strasseanzug (Walking Out Dress)
Mütze
Waffenrock or Uberrock
Shoulder cords
Short white or brown gloves
White linen or blue/black trousers
Boots with screwed on spurs
Degen (undress sword)
Paletot or Umhang

Gala Anzug fur Tänzende (Dress for Festive Dances and Balls)
Helmet with parade eagle
Gala Waffenrock
Epaulettes
Gorget
Short white gloves
Order and decorations
Gala trousers
Boots with screwed on spurs
Degen

Kleiner Dienstanzug (Undress Uniform for Duty Occasions)
Helmet or Mütze
Koller or Waffenrock
Shoulder cords
Short brown gloves
Trousers with boots with screwed on spurs or riding breeches and
  jackboots

Sabre or Degen
Paletot, Mantel or Umhang
(Dress depending on the Order of the Day)

Dienstanzug (Duty Dress)
Helmet (with cover if men wear covers)
Waffenrock or koller
Shoulder cords
Gorget
Feldbinde, the Adjutant wore the shoulder sash
Pouch belt and pouch (the adjutant did not wear these)
Short white or grey gloves
Ribbons on the waffenrock, orders and decorations on the koller
Riding breeches and jack boots
Sabre
Paletot

Hofgarten Anzug (Dress for Palace Garden Parties)
Mütze
Waffenrock
Shoulder cords
Gorget
Orders and decorations
White linen trousers
Boots with screwed on spurs

Kürassier-Offizere
(shown here for comparison with the Garde du Corps Orders of Dress)
Paradeanzug (Parade Dress)
Helmet, with parade eagle for Guard Regiment
Koller
Cuirass
Pouch and pouch bandolier
Gauntlets
Gorget trophy or smaller version on breast of cuirass
Sash
Riding breeches and jack boots
Sabre

Gesellschaftanzug (Dress for Social Occasions)
Helmet (chin scales up)
Waffenrock
Epaulettes
Gorget for 1st and 2nd Regts
Short white gloves
Black/blue trousers
Boots with screwed on spurs
Degen

Hofballanzug (fur Tänze) (Dress for Palace Balls)
Helmet (with chin scales up) Parade eagle for the Guard Regiment
Koller
Orders and decorations
Sword belt over koller
Sabre (hooked up)
Gala trousers

Boots with screwed on spurs
Epaulettes
Dienstanzug (Duty Dress)
Helmet with chin scales down
Waffenrock or Uberrock (the latter with the skirts hooked up)
Shoulder cords
Pouch belt and pouch
Feldbinde (Adjutant with sash over shoulder but without pouch or belt)
Riding breeches and jack boots
Sabre
Mantel with pouch belt and Feldbinde over when troops wear the mantel
Ausgehenun (Walking Out Dress)
Mütze
Waffenrock or Uberrock
Shoulder cords
White or brown gloves
White linen trousers or black/blue trousers
Degen
Boots with screwed on spurs
Dienstanzug auf Truppenübungsplatz (Duty Dress on the Barracks Square)
Mütze
Litewka
White or black/blue trousers
Boots with screwed on spurs
Reitanzug (Riding Dress)
Mütze
Uberrock with skirts folded back
Brown gloves
Riding breeches and jack boots or black/blue trousers with boots with
  screwed on spurs

BELOW, LEFT: Officers' pattern helmet, Gardes du Corps with special parade eagle. BELOW, RIGHT: Troopers' pattern helmet, Gardes du Corps. Note smaller and lower pattern skull piece.

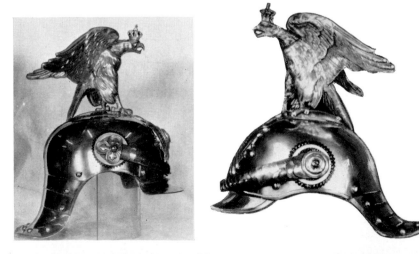

30

ABOVE: SM Kaiser Wilhelm II in the Parade Uniform of the Gardes du Corps. The helmet has a special pattern silver-plated eagle with a gilt crown, and the helmet plate is inlaid with black, orange and gilded enamel (Radio Times Hutton Picture Library).

Helme (Helmets)

The helmet was tombak with German Silver mountings and a German Silver 'Guard Star' plate with tombak centre. For parades and ceremonial occasions the spike was removed and replaced by an imposing silver eagle, 'wings outspread as if to spring from the top of the helmet, it's beak open and the head surmounted by the Prussian crown.' The officers' pattern eagle had a gilded crown, and their helmets were generally decorated with silver mounts, the front plate having an enamelled centre in orange, black green and gold. The step in the officers' helmet visors was very pronounced and the other ranks pattern had a much lower and smaller skull part. The helmet plate design is described fully under the section on the Guard Cuirassier Regiment helmet.

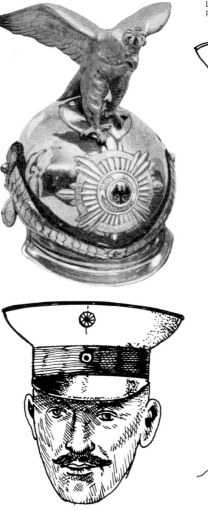

LEFT: Front view of the official pattern helmet, Gardes du Corps.

Mütze worn with walking out dress.

Officers pattern mütze

Mütze worn with barrack and fatigue dress.

Mütze (Undress Cap)

White with a red band and red upper piping. Cockades and black peaks for the senior NCO's and officers as for the line regiments.

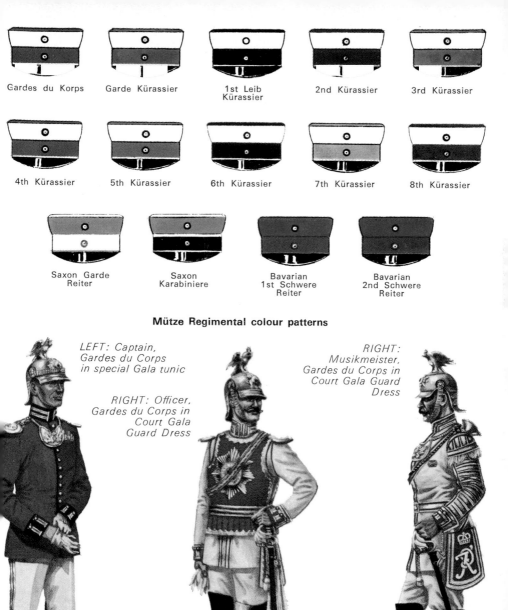

Gardes du Korps	Garde Kürassier	1st Leib Kürassier	2nd Kürassier	3rd Kürassier

4th Kürassier	5th Kürassier	6th Kürassier	7th Kürassier	8th Kürassier

Saxon Garde Reiter	Saxon Karabiniere	Bavarian 1st Schwere Reiter	Bavarian 2nd Schwere Reiter

Mütze Regimental colour patterns

LEFT: Captain, Gardes du Corps in special Gala tunic

RIGHT: Officer, Gardes du Corps in Court Gala Guard Dress

RIGHT: Musikmeister, Gardes du Corps in Court Gala Guard Dress

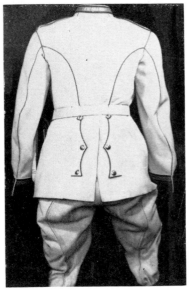

ABOVE: Detail views of the collar and cuff, on an NCO's pattern Koller of the Guard Regiment. Note Guard pattern NCO's lace and 'Litzen'. RIGHT: Front and rear view of the Koller with reinforced strapping on the breeches.

Koller (Full Dress Tunic)

Yellow-white kirsey tunics (an NCO's pattern cuirassier tunic examined in the Imperial War Museum reveals little if any of this yellow-white colour. It appears to be white face-cloth but may of course be a custom made tunic bought privately) as for the line regiments with red collars and cuffs and red piping in the seams and on the pockets. Red and white tunic braid (silver and red for the officers). The collar and cuffs decorated

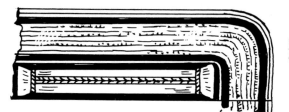

LEFT: Tunic border for officers' of the Gardes du Corps.

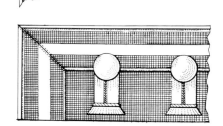

RIGHT: Guard loop (Litzen) worn on collar of tunic and edge of cuff. BELOW, LEFT TO RIGHT: NCO's collar button; 1st Squadron; Leib-Kompanie Gardes du Corps.

with white (silver for the officers) square ended loops of lace known as 'Garde Litzen'.

The loops were placed one each side of the collar fronts and two on each cuff. NCO's tunics distinguished by a strip of lozenge figured silver lace along the central stripe of the collar and cuffs of the tunic braid besides the heraldic buttons. The 'Wachtmeister' had an additional

*Adjutant, Garde—
Kürassier Regiment
in Waffenrock and Mütze*

*Trooper, Garde—
Kürassier Regiment
in Parade Dress. Note
2nd class Fechtabzeichen
on right arm*

*Major, Garde—
Kürassier Regiment in
special Gala tunic*

rooper, 4th Kürassier
Regiment in Koller

N.C.O., Saxon Garde,
Reiter Regiment
in Parade Dress

Trumpeter, Saxon
Karabinier Regiment
in Parade Dress

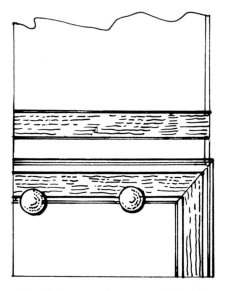

Detail of Etatsmässiger Wacht-meisters' tunic cuff with extra braiding to indicate rank. Line Regiment).

strip of the same lace around the sleeve above each cuff. Trumpeters had a double row of similar patterned but narrower lace on the collar and cuffs and on the red shoulder wings. The 'Leib-Kompanie' had an 'L' on their shoulder strap buttons. The remaining squadrons an Arabic numeral.

Waffenrock (Undress Tunic)

A very dark blue, single breasted tunic, with red collar patches and red cuffs and with red piping down the front of the leading edge of the coat and on the pocket flaps. The collar and cuffs decorated with 'Gardelitzen' in a similar fashion to the full dress tunic. The collar and the cuffs further decorated with the full dress tunic braid, German Silver buttons. The officers' coats had the whole of the collar coloured red and had silver and red tunic border on the collar and cuffs. NCO's and Trumpeters had their rank distinctions on the collar and cuffs and on the wings. The rank and file had white shoulder straps edged with red piping and buttons as on the 'Koller', and the officers wore the shoulder cords which passed through silver and black bridles and were lined with red underlay.

Uberrock (Officers' Frock Coat)

Very dark blue coat in the Prussian style with red collar, breast linings and pipings and silver buttons.

Paletot/Mantel/Umhang (Officers' Overcoats and Cloaks)

The same pattern as the line regiments with collars, red when turned up and white with a red piping when folded down.

Mantel (NCO and Troopers' Overcoats)

As line regiments with German Silver buttons, red collar patches with two Garde-Litzen (each having a red 'light', and white shoulder

ABOVE: Standartenträger and NCO of the Gardes du Corps. The Kaiser's personal escort. Reputed to be the tallest men in German Army at that time, the man on the right was 6 feet 7 inches without his helmet.

straps edged with red piping. The NCO's white, black striped distinguishing strips on the collar patches laid horizontal above the lace bars (two bars for the Wachtmeister the second bar beneath the lace bars).

Litewka (Working Tunics)

The same pattern as the line regiments. The officers' collar patches

Officer, 1st Leib—
Kürassier Regiment
in Parade Dress

Einjährige Freiwillige,
7th Kürassier Regiment
in Waffenrock with
Fechtabzeichen,
Flaggenwinkenabzeichen
and Schützenabzeichen

Officer, 8th Kürassier
Regiment in Paletot

Officer, 5th Kürassier
Regiment in
Waffenrock

Trumpet Major of the
6th Kürassier Regiment

were white with red piping and the rest of the piping on the coat the same colour. Buttons silver. The NCO's and troopers coats had red collar patches with the guard lace bars as on the overcoat. The Wachtmeister had a silver, three chevron badge on the left upper sleeve.

Kürasse (Cuirass)

The Life Guards' breast and back plates were steel but faced with brass and joined over the shoulders with ornate hinges decorated with double brass chains. From 1912 a small trophy comprising the centre decoration of the gorget was worn placed on the upper part of the breast plate between the hinges.

For New Year's Parades (by order, but certainly on other occasions according to photographs) the old traditional black iron cuirass was worn with scarlet cord trimming. In 1897, to commemorate the anniversary of the birth of William I, the Kaiser presented the regiment with new black polished iron cuirasses all with the same scarlet cord trimming. From 1912 the gorget trophy was worn on the black cuirasses.

Kartuschekasten (Pouch)

Black polished leather with a German Silver Guard Star ornament on the lid. The officers' pattern had a silver ornament.

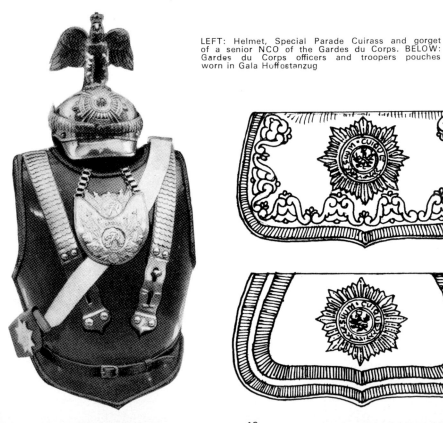

LEFT: Helmet, Special Parade Cuirass and gorget of a senior NCO of the Gardes du Corps. BELOW: Gardes du Corps officers and troopers pouches worn in Gala Huffostanzug

Epauletten (Epaulettes)

The same pattern as for the line regiments but with a silver cloth shoulder board and silver crescents all on a red underlay.

Brustchilder (Gorgets)

From January 24, 1912 the regiment wore gorgets. These large and elegant brass breast ornaments had a central white metal cartouche surrounded by trophies of flags, kettledrums and swords in the baroque style with a large crown overall and the FR cypher in the central tablet surrounded by sprays of palm and with a further small cartouche below, bearing the initial 'W' with a crown over and II beneath.

For the NCO's the central cartouche was gilded and for the officers the centre was enamelled red with a gilt cypher, the trophies were silver and the gorget was trimmed in silver. The ornament was worn, suspended on a brass, flat linked chain, the officers used a fine linked chain on red cloth.

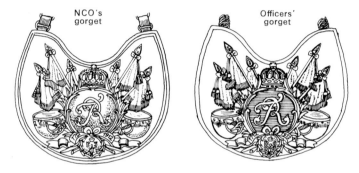

NCO's gorget

Officers' gorget

Gala Waffenrock (Officers' Tunic for Festive Occasions)

A red, single breasted tunic with a high, dark blue collar cut square and hooked close in front, dark blue cuffs and blue piping. Buttons silver. The collar fronts and cuffs decorated with silver lace, two bars on each collar front in this case. The coat was lined with white silk.

Langetuchehosen (Undress Trousers)

Dark blue with red stripes.

Gala Tuchhosen
(Officers' Special Trousers for Festive Occasions)

White with a stripe of the tunic braid down each outside leg.

Reithosen/Reitsteifel (Riding Breeches and Boots)

White kirsey riding breeches with leather strapping and black boots as for line cuirassiers.

Feldbinde (Waistbelt)

Silver with two black stripes and a silver round locket and clasp buckle. The belt was edged on its upper and lower edges with red and the slides similarly decorated from 1897.

*Etatsmässige
Wachtmeister, 3rd
Kürassier Regiment in
Koller. Note report book
carried in the front of
the tunic*

*Adjutant,
7th Kürassier Regiment
in Mantel*

*Trumpeter, 1st Bavarian
Schweres Reiter
Regiment*

Officer, 2nd Bavarian
Schweres Reiter
Regiment

Trumpeter, 1st Troop
Prussian Leibgendarmerie

NCO Gardarme, 2nd
Troop Prussian
Leibgendarmerie

Schabrake/Schabrunken (Housings and Wallet Flaps)

For parades, red housings and wallet flaps were used. The housing, which passed right under the saddle was cut almost rectangular and edged with a double band of worsted cloth, the outer narrow, the inner broad, separated by a narrow 'light' and with an outer red piping on the edge. The worsted bands for the NCO's and troopers were white and the 'light' between the bands red. For the officers the decorative bands were silver lace with a black velvet 'light' between. In the rear corners of the housing and on each wallet flap was the ubiquitous Star of the Order of the Black Eagle (the Guard Star) in this case surmounted by

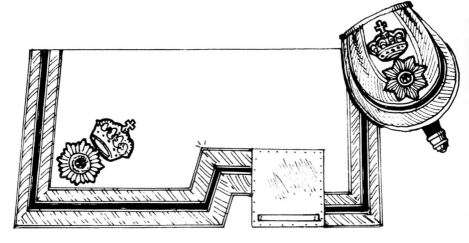

ABOVE: Housing and wallet flaps used by officers of the Gardes du Corps. The leather panel is to protect the cloth when the saddle was placed over this the girth strap passed through the loops. RIGHT: Troopers wallet flap of Gardes du Corps.

the crown. The crowns on the housing were set on at angles and those on the flaps upright. The NCO's and troopers stars were white and those of the officers silver, the crowns silver also. The NCO's and troopers had yellow crowns. The wallet flaps differed in design for the officers and the rank and file. The officers' pattern had splayed sides and a curved lower edge, the rank and file pattern hexagonal with the point at the bottom. On the officers' pattern the star covered the inner lace band.

Pauken (Kettledrums)

In 1810 the regiment were awarded the distinction of carrying the kettledrums of the former Kürassier Regiment No 12.

Standartenträger (Standard Bearer)

Bandolier faced with poppy red velvet, edged with silver lace and with silver fringing. The Guard pattern standard bearers gorget was worn, below the regimental gorget when the cuirass was not worn, but above the gorget trophy on the breast when the cuirass was worn.

LEFT: Standartenträger of the Gardes du Corp wearing the standard Gorget apparently without the usual armshield. He also wears the special parade eagle on his helmet in place of the usual spike.

Standard bearer of the Gardes du Corps in Special Parade Dress. Note the armshield and gorget standard is shown in detail on page 65

48

Kesselpauker (Kettledrummer)
Long silver fringing on wings.

Hoffestanzug (Court Ceremonial Dress)
The 'Gardes du Corps' ceremonial duty at Court was restricted to specially selected officers, NCO's and troopers of the 'Leib-Kompanie' and the Trumpet Corps. For this special duty a series of specially designed uniform items were worn.

Troopers' and officers' Gala Hoffestanzug

Supraveste
This was worn over the full dress tunic and comprised a short skirted, round necked, crimson vest known as the 'drawing-room cuirass', with a pleated skirt and fastened under the left arm by a number of hooks and eyes. The vest was bordered, for the NCO's and troopers, by a wide white worsted braid with a narrow red piping on the edge. On the breast and the back were white embroidered Stars of the Order of The Black Eagle with a red (originally orange) centre circle bearing the black heraldic Prussian eagle with yellow crown, beak, talons, sword and thunderbolts. Around this circle a white circular band lettered 'SUUM CUIQUE' in yellow embroidery picked out black and with two sprays of laurel (with red fruit) beneath the lettering. The officers' pattern was crimson velvet edged and decorated with a rich, leaf pattern, silver lace. The front and rear stars were padded and raised and richly embroidered in silver and coloured silks. They wore the sash over the vest and the epaulettes beneath it.

Sword Belt, Bandolier and Sabretache
For the rank and file and the NCO's these items were white lacquered leather decorated on either side with a strip of crimson-red worsted braid and with silvered mountings. The pouch lid was also lacquered

LEFT: Officers'
pattern sabretache
RIGHT: Troopers'
pattern sabretache

white and decorated with an edging of the tunic braid and with the Guard Star as its central ornament. From 1883 a sabretache was worn, supported on narrow white leather straps and worn high on the left hip. The sabretache was faced with red cloth, edged with a double border of tunic braid and with an 'FR' cypher and crown as a central motif. The crown was embellished with red and green 'stones' on its brow band.

The officers' belts, pouch lid (the pouch itself was white) and sabretache were red Moroccan leather faced with red velvet and decorated in rich silver embroidery. The pouch lid had a central silver star and the sabretache a silver crown and 'FR' cypher. The pouch bandolier was worn over the vest.

Trumpeter

The 'supraveste' was not worn. The pouch, bandolier and sabretache were the troopers' pattern. Short gloves were worn instead of gauntlets. A special full dress 'Koller' was decorated throughout with silver NCO's lace, the shoulder straps were also decorated with silver and the sleeves had 11 horizontal silver, red edged, lacings right round with a similar vertical lace up the front and down the back of the sleeve. The wings were white and were decorated with similar pattern lace set on vertically.

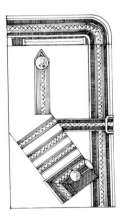

LEFT: Gala Dress, Trumpeter Gardes du Corps shown in schematic form.

The Trumpet Corps of the Gardes du Corps in Parade Dress

Strabstrompeter/Pauker

The tunic braid was 1·8 cm wide and in silver and red as worn by the trumpeter. There were 12 bars on each sleeve, the upper two being under the long silver fringing on the wings. The guard lace on the collar and cuffs was white silk and the bandolier and the pouch were decorated with silver edged red lace. In 1908 the 'Musikmeister' continued to wear this dress. The uniform was completed by white wash leather breeches and high patent leather jackboots with silvered spurs.

The helmet with the parade eagle was worn with this dress.

Trumpet Banner

A red rectangular trumpet banner with silver fringe, central silver Guard Star and a gold crown in each corner. The centre of the Star in coloured silks.

PRUSSIAN CUIRASSIER REGIMENTS

Helme (Helmet)

The metal, spiked helmet of the German cuirassier was first taken into use in 1842. Several patterns followed, the penultimate being the M 1889, first approved by an order of January 1889 and worn until the adoption of the steel spiked helmet in 1916.

In design the helmet resembled the basic shape of the 17th century lobster-tailed English pot helmet and traditional Polish 'zischaagge'.

The cuirassier helmet was polished steel except for the Guard Regiment and the 6th Regiment who adopted tombak helmets (Tombak being an alloy of copper and zinc, its name derived from the Portuguese word 'Tambaca'). The helmet had a swept out front visor and a deep curving segmented rear visor forming a neck guard. The NCO's and troopers pattern had a rounded and flattened front visor, the officers' pattern cut square and having a pronounced lateral ridge or step. The visors of the officers' helmets were painted a flat-green on the underside, those of the NCO's and troopers black.

The steel helmets had brass mountings, the tombak helmets mountings in German Silver. The column and collar of the spikes were brass for the steel helmet, the spike itself being steel. The tombak helmets had spike column and collars in steel, the spike itself being tombak. The

TOP LEFT: Officers' pattern Helmet, Line Kürassier Regiment TOP RIGHT: Troopers' pattern helmet, Garde Kürassier Regiment (Wallis and Wallis). BOTTOM LEFT: Line Kürassier helmet. Note chin scale boss, cockade and circular vent to spike column. CENTRE AND BOTTOM RIGHT: Two views of a troopers' pattern helmet—Garde-Kürassier Regiment (Tradition).

NCO's and troopers had spikes of a simple squat conical design, the columns vented by a small hole in the sides. The officers' helmets had taller, hexagonal fluted spikes (of varying heights) and had columns vented with stylised crosses. Officers' helmets had the plate at the base of the spike column in a cross design, the NCO's and troopers pattern having a simpler and oval base plate.

For parade and ceremonial duties the Guard Regiment wore a German Silver crowned eagle in lieu of the spike. The officers' pattern eagle was silver and its crown was gilded. This eagle was the same design as the Gardes du Corps parade eagle.

Chin straps were covered in brass scales for all steel and tombak helmets. The scales of the officers' helmets were gilded. The bosses from which the scales were suspended were situated on the sides of the helmets and differed in design for Officers and NCO's and troopers. The officers' pattern were ornate trefoils and for the NCO's and troopers a plain circular type boss with a raised rim and a central fluted rivet was adopted. Generally the scales were convex and scalloped but the Officers of the 1st Regiment adopted a special and simpler flat pattern with semi-circular scale plates.

BOTTOM LEFT: A troopers' model Line Kürassier helmet early pattern. BOTTOM, RIGHT: Line Kürassier helmet—the all steel pattern issued in 1916. (Tradition). TOP, LEFT: An officers' pattern helmet. Line Kürassier Regiment. TOP, RIGHT: Officer's pattern helmet, 2nd Kürassier Regiment.

LEFT: Helmet plates of the Leib Kürassier Regiment. (Top) Officers' pattern. (Bottom) Troopers' pattern. ABOVE: Helmet plate of a Line Kürassier Regiment.

LEFT: Officers' pattern helmet plate, Garde Kürassier Regiment. BELOW, LEFT: Troopers' pattern, Garde Kürassier Regiment. BELOW RIGHT: Helmet plate of the 2nd Kürassier Regiment.

Behind each chin scale boss a metal cockade was worn. On the right side the black, white and red 'Reichkokarde' and on the left the 'Prussian' black and white cockade. Officers of the 1st Regiment carried the 'Old Hessian' cockade, that is to say, black with a silver edge and centre. The officers' cockades were better quality, deeper chiselled and enamelled.

The fronts of the helmets were decorated with a 'helmet plate'. With the exception of the Guard and 1st Regiments this comprised the Prussian heraldic eagle clutching the sceptre in its right talon and the orb in its left. Across the upper breast a three section motto scroll inscribed 'MIT GOTT/FUR KÖNIG/UND VATERLAND' and beneath the scroll, on the eagle's breast, the initials 'FR'. In addition the 2nd Regiment had a second, wider scroll over the lower part of the eagle's body lettered 'Hohenfriedberg 4 Juni 1745'. Versions exist with an alternative spelling of König—'Koenig'.

In 1902 the 1st Regiment adopted a special helmet plate comprising the 'Old Brandenberg' Prussian Eagle, flying to its left and clutching a cross-hilted sword in its right talons and a bundle of thunderbolts in its left. Across the wings, over the crowned head, a curved scroll bearing the words 'PRO GLORIA ET PATRIA'.

The Guard Cuirassier Regiment wore the eight pointed Guard Star with a circular motto band inscribed 'MIT GOTT/FUR KÖNIG/UND VATER/LAND/1860', the scroll woven in and out of the flanges of the star. The middle circlet was bordered by a further motto band lettered 'SUUM CUIQUE' with two crossed laurel branches below the wording and in its centre the Black Prussian Eagle. The officers' plate was silvered with a richly enamelled centre in orange, black, green and gold, that of the NCO's and troopers in German Silver with a red and black centre.

From 1892 helmets were furnished with 'reed' green cloth covers for manoeuvres and other field exercises. This cover known as the 'manöverkappe' was given a red band dividing it in two parts from 1908. It carried no number and had a number of vent holes around the base of the spike.

  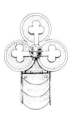

LEFT: Kürassier officers' chinscale
RIGHT: Kürassier NCO's and troopers' chinscale

RIGHT: Officers' chinscale Kürassier Regiment No 1

Mütze (The Undress Cap)

This headdress was worn for walking out, undress, working dress and for some drills. For troopers and junior NCO's the cap was peakless. Senior NCO's and the officers wore caps with small black gutta percha or leather peaks. The upper part of the cap was white and the brow band and the piping around the crown were in the regimental facing colour.

On the front of the cap were two cockades, on the lower band the Prussian cockade—black, white, black and on the upper, white section the 'Reichkokarde', red, (in the centre) white and black. Officers of the 2nd Regiment had black velvet cap bands and piping.

LEFT: Officers' undress cap being worn with the überrock. BELOW: Officer and Elätsmassige Wachtmeister in undress caps. Note report book tucked in the front of the Wachtmeisters' Koller. OPPOSITE PAGE: Exercise parade of a Line Kürassier Regiment in undress caps. Note the trumpeter at right and the visored cap and Fechterabzeichen on the arm of the first man in the centre rank.

Kürasse (Cuirass)

The cuirass comprised a breast and back plate and was generally of polished steel. The two plates were connected by two long hinges, riveted on the back plate, hinged at the shoulder and coming well down over the breast plate to which they were retained by long studs. The hinges were backed by leather and there was a black leather belt, riveted on either side of the back plate and coming round to the front of the breast plate where it was fastened by a small buckle. The left shoulder hinge had a small hook which facilitated the retention of the cartridge pouch bandolier. The extremities of the officers' 'hinges' were decorated

with lions heads (on the back plate) and an oak leaf design (on the breast plate ends). Both plates weighed approximately 10 kilogramms and were worn only for 'Paradeanzug', mounted parades and honour duties. In winter the cuirass was worn over the overcoats by both officers and NCO's and troopers.

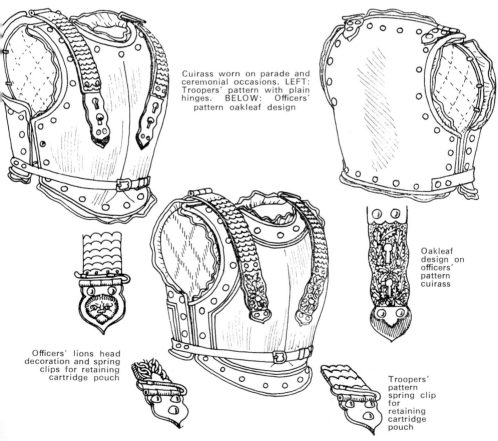

Cuirass worn on parade and ceremonial occasions. LEFT: Troopers' pattern with plain hinges. BELOW: Officers' pattern oakleaf design

Oakleaf design on officers' pattern cuirass

Officers' lions head decoration and spring clips for retaining cartridge pouch

Troopers' pattern spring clip for retaining cartridge pouch

Officers' pattern
cuirass

Troopers' cuirass
1st Regiment

Troopers' cuirass 2nd Regiment

THE GARDE KÜRASSIER REGT

Breast and back plates plated with tombak.

2ND AND 6TH REGIMENTS

Officers and NCO's had the breast and back plates plated with tombak.

RIGHT: Officers of a Line Kürassier Regiment in cuirass, scabbards are 'browned' FOOT OF PAGE: Officers of a Line Kürassier Regiment in cuirasses. Note Regimental Standard in background.

1ST REGIMENT

Officers had the breast and back plates decorated with gilded rims and silver plated studding, and the central trophy of the regimental gorget on the breast plate for all ranks.

2ND REGIMENT

All ranks carried a version of the regimental gorget on the breast plate.

ABOVE LEFT: Kronprinz Wilhelm in the uniform of the 2nd Regiment. ABOVE RIGHT: Officer and NCO of a Line Regiment in cuirasses. Note Fechterabzeichen on nearest man's arm. ABOVE: Schützen-Schnur, worn over the cuirass.

The officers' cuirasses were lined with quilted white silk and the NCO's and troopers patterns with grey linen.

The officers had a black velvet ruffling or edging around the neck and arm holes edged with white cord piping and the NCO's and troopers a coarse black cloth trimming similarly decorated.

The pouch belt was worn over the cuirass passing under the right side hinge and under the narrow waist belt thereby preventing it from moving when the wearer was mounted.

The 'shützen-schnur' was worn from the left shoulder looped down to the front extremity of the left 'hinge'.

Decorations were also worn on the lower part of the left hinge. See under the heading Standartenträger as to how the gorget of the appointment was worn in relation to the regimental devices by the 1st and 2nd Regiments.

Koller (The Full Dress Tunic)

The distinctive tunic of the cuirassier regiments was first taken into use in 1842 along with the spiked helmet. The NCO's and troopers' tunic was made in coarse weave, kirsey material which produced a yellowish-white appearance. The officers wore tunics of fine white melton facing cloth (see note under Garde du Corps tunic regarding colour).

The tunic had the collar fronts and Swedish pattern cuffs in the regimental facing colour with similar coloured pipings in the arm seams, around the seam of the arm hole, in the back seams, along the edges of the skirt pockets and around the white shoulder straps.

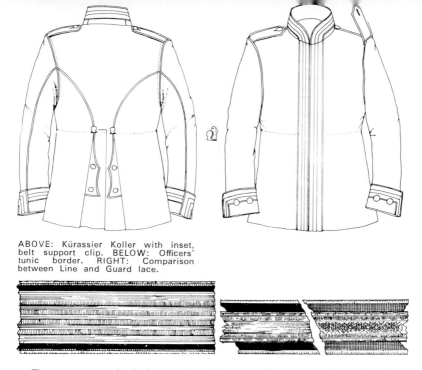

ABOVE: Kürassier Koller with inset, belt support clip. BELOW: Officers' tunic border. RIGHT: Comparison between Line and Guard lace.

The coat was single breasted, with a standing, round fronted collar, hooked close down the front with approximately sixteen hooks and eyes. The officers' coats had twenty-two hooks and eyes. The Swedish pattern cuffs had two flat buttons on each and three similar buttons on the skirt pocket flaps and on the shoulder straps. The top buttons on the pockets were modified to support the waist belt and the shoulder buttons carried the squadron number. Officers' buttons were gilt or silvered, those of the NCO's and troopers brass or 'Britannia' metal.

The tunic was trimmed with the so-called 'kollerborte' (tunic border) along the top edge and fronts of the collar and down each coat front to the bottom edge of the skirts and along the top and rear edge of the cuffs. This braid consisted of a wide strip of white linen on which two bands of the facing cloth were stitched and so placed as to show a white central stripe and two white, narrow edges. The 3rd Regiment had a special braid called the 'Old Brandenburg' pattern which comprised two outer stripes of light blue braid with a white worsted lace strip down the centre decorated with woven light blue lozenges.

The tunics of the NCO's were distinguished by a 1·2 cm wide gold or silver patterned lace stitched over the central white strip of the collar and cuff tunic braid.

The tunics of the officers were decorated with a tunic border which comprised a band of flat, and raised, silver or gold lace with two narrow silk stripes of the facing colour worked along each edge. Their epaulettes were retained by 'passanten' (keepers or bridles) of silver, black striped lace lined with the facing colour.

The tunics of the officers were lined throughout with white silk except

61

ABOVE: Quarter-guard of a Line Kürassier Regiment in Koller and 1888 model jackboots. All carry the standard pallasch or sabre.

for the officers of the 1st Regiment who had black linings. The NCO's and troopers' coats had grey calico linings.

The Guard Regiment had square ended loops of white (silver for officers) 'Guard lace' on the collar fronts and on the cuffs (one loop on each collar front and two on each cuff).

Regiments with regimental 'chefs' wore distinctive badges on the epaulettes and shoulder straps. These were as follows:

1st Regiment	Crown over 'WR' Cypher
2nd Regiment	Crown over 'L'
6th Regiment	Crown over Russian cyrillic 'N' and 'I'
8th Regiment	Crown over 'GR' and Roman figure 'V'

these ornaments were in the facing colour for the NCO's and troopers of the 2nd Regiment and yellow for all the other Regiments, and in diecast or moulded gold or silver for the officers.

NCO's and troopers' shoulder strap devices

Officers' Regimental shoulder devices in moulded gold or silver worn on the epaulettes and the shoulder cords.

The sleeves of the full dress tunic were made long and fell well over the hand to the knuckles. When worn on manoeuvres or for field exercise the longish skirts hooked back to reveal the linings.

Regiment	Facings and Pipings	Buttons
Gardes du Corps	Poppy Red	White
Guard Regiment	Cornflower Blue	White
1st Regt	Black	Yellow
2nd Regt	Crimson Red	White
3rd Regt	Light Blue	White
4th Regt	Vermillion Red	White
5th Regt	Rose Red	Yellow
6th Regt	Russian Blue	Yellow
7th Regt	Lemon Yellow	White
8th Regt	Sea Green	Yellow

Officers of the 1st Regiment had Black Velvet facings, the 4th Vermillion, the Rose Red of the 5th was a soft rich pink, the Russian Blue of the 6th Regiment a beautiful dark ultramarine, the Yellow of the 7th a bright lemon colour and the facings of the 8th Regiment a rich Sea Green. The crimson facings of the officers of the 2nd Regiment were a lighter shade than the NCO's and troopers facing colours.

BELOW: Koller worn on field exercises. This was the standard method for transporting horses across deep water when no bridges were available.

Kürassier waffenrock

Waffenrock (The Undress Tunic)

The undress cuirassier tunic was a dark blue, single breasted coat with a standing collar and Swedish cuffs. The coat had eight flat (domed for officers) buttons down the front, two on each cuff, one on each shoulder (with the squadron number) and three on each pocket flap, the upper two of a special design to support the sword belt.

NCO's and troopers had collar patches and cuffs in the facing colour (poppy red for the 6th Regiment), and the officers' coats had the whole

BELOW: Officers of the 8th Regiment in the waffenrock. Note slack pouch belt of officer second from right.

Standard of the Gardes du Corps. The staff has been turned a quarter of a turn to the right (viewed from the rear) to show the eagle in profile. Note the Commemorative Campaign Streamers detailed on page 110.

ABOVE: Kronprinz Wilhelm in waffenrock with riding breeches and jackboots. FOOT OF PAGE: This view shows clearly the differences between the waffenrock worn by the officer on the left and the Koller, with skirts hooked back worn by the two orderlies on the right.

collar and the cuffs in the facing colour. The collars and cuffs of the tunic were trimmed with the tunic braid as worn on the koller (yellow and red braid for the 6th Regiment, gold and red for their officers).

Officers usually, but not always wore the shoulder cords with this coat, retained by buttons and by small silver, black striped, bridles, and the NCO's and troopers had the white point-ended shoulder straps with a piping in the facing colour as worn on the full dress tunic (edged red until 1903 and blue thereafter by the 6th Regiment).

Collars and cuffs were piped with blue (except for the Guard Regiment which had red pipings and the 1st Regiment which had white). Regiments with special devices on the shoulder strap continued to wear these on the undress tunic.

The officers of the Guard Regiment had red linings to their coats, the other regiments white.

Officers' coats were provided with a slit on the left side through which the undress sword could be worn. The 'feldbinde' was worn over this coat. Officers of the Guard Regiment also wore a special gala waffenrock for duties at court and at levees. The coat was red with cornflower blue collar and cuffs and white pipings. The collar fronts were each decorated with two bars of silver Garde-litzen and there were two further loops on each cuff. The collar of the coat was high, and cut square in front and the coat was lined with white silk. The coat had silver buttons.

WAFFENROCK FACING DETAIL

Regiment	Collar	Cuffs	Buttons	Piping	Shoulder Strap Device for NCO's & troopers
Garde du Corps	Red with white or silver lace bars	Red with white or silver lace bars	White	Red	-
Guard Kürassier Regt	Cornflower Blue with white or silver lace bars	Cornflower Blue with white or silver lace bars	White	Red	-
1st Regt (Black velvet facings)	Black	Black	Yellow	White	Yellow
2nd Regt	Crimson Red	Crimson Red	White	Red	Red
3rd Regt	Light Blue	Light Blue	White	Light Blue	-
4th Regt	Vermillion Red	Vermillion Red	White	Red	-
5th Regt	Rose Red	Rose Red	Yellow	Rose	-
6th Regt	Poppy Red	Poppy Red	Yellow	Poppy Red	Yellow
7th Regt	Lemon Yellow	Lemon Yellow	White	Yellow	-
8th Regt	Sea Green	Sea Green	Yellow	White	Yellow

LEFT: Standard of the Garde
Kürassier.

RIGHT: Regimental
Standard of the 1st Leib
Kürassier Regiment.

LEFT: Life Standard of the 1st
Leib Kürassier Regiment.

LEFT: *Standard of Kürassier Regiment No 2.*

RIGHT: *Standard of Kürassier Regiment No 3.*

LEFT: *Standard of Kürassier Regiment No 4.*

69

Various ways of wearing the waffen-rock. BELOW: Officers of the Gardes du Corps in waffenrock. Note Feld-binde. ABOVE, LEFT: Officer of the 8th Regiment in waffenrock with helmet. Note Feldbinde and brown gloves. ABOVE: Officer of the 8th Regiment wearing waffenrock under the paletot and with the undress cap.

ABOVE: Officers of a Line Kürassier Regiment in überrock. Note the method of carrying the sabre.

Überrock (The Officers' Frock Coat)

The officers' frock was a blue double breasted coat with two rows of six buttons down the fronts. The cuffs were deep and a plain round design and in the rear there was a slit to the waist level with two triangular vertical pockets on either side, each flap fitted with two buttons. The coat reached to a hand's width below the knees and the skirts were supplied with hooks and eyes so that they could be hooked back, if required. The cuirassier frock coat was a particularly dark shade of blue and had the collar in the facing colour except for the 6th Regiment, which had poppy red. The insides of the breasts were in the facing colour and the edges of the cuffs and the pocket flaps were also piped with the facing colour. The coat had a slit in the left side through which the undress sword hilt protruded when the sword was worn under the coat.

Regiment	Collar	Piping	Buttons
Gardes du Corps	Red	Red	Silver
Garde Kürassier Regt	Cornflower Blue piped red	Red	Silver
1st Regt	Black piped white	White	Gold
2nd Regt	Red piped blue	White on cuffs	Silver
3rd Regt*	Light Blue	Light Blue on pockets, white on cuffs	Silver
4th Regt	Red	Red	Silver
5th Regt	Rose Red	Rose Red	Gold
6th Regt	Poppy Red	Poppy Red	Gold
7th Regt	Yellow piped blue	Yellow	Silver
8th Regt	Green piped white	White	White

* Note that one German authority gives the 3rd Regiment Light Blue piping on the cuffs also.

LEFT: Standard of Kürassier
Regiment No 5.

RIGHT: Standard of
Kürassier Regiment
No 6.

LEFT: Standard of Kürassier
Regiment No 7, pre 1903.

LEFT: Standard of Kürassier Regiment No 7, post 1903.

RIGHT: Standard of Kürassier Regiment No 8.

LEFT: Standard of 1st Bavarian Schweres Reiter Regiment.

Mantel/Paletot (Officers' Greatcoats)

The old Prussian overcoat was a grey (in some cases very dark in colour) single-breasted garment which reached almost to the ground and was covered to finger tip length with a cloak known as a 'pelerine'. After the formation of the new 'German' army a coat, sometimes referred to as the 'Hohenzollern' overcoat was introduced.

The new overcoat was light grey (in some cases very pale grey), double breasted with two rows of six, regimentally coloured buttons down the front and a 20-28 inch long slit at the rear which could be closed by three or four small horn buttons. The two coats differed in that the mantel was primarily intended as the garment for mounted duties and the paletot for wear on foot. When not on duty the officer had the choice of either garment. For winter parades the cuirass was worn over the mantel with the bandolier and the pouch over it. The collar of both coats was the folded-down variety and made so that it could be worn up, or down. A table of the colours of the collars is shown below from which it will be seen that the facing colour appeared when the collar was turned up. From 1893 General officers wore the grey overcoats but with special red pipings on the edges of the cuffs, pocket flaps and slits.

Regiment	Collar folded down	Collar turned up
2nd Regt	Dark Blue	Crimson
3rd Regt	Dark Blue	Light Blue
4th Regt	Dark Blue	Red
5th Regt	Dark Blue	Rose Red
6th Regt	Dark Blue	Poppy Red
7th Regt	Dark Blue	Yellow
8th Regt	Dark Blue	Green piped white

ABOVE: Officer in überrock with skirts hooked back and wearing the undress cap. Note the white breech and long boots and the detail of the officer's bridle.

Paletot (note slit in left side for sword suspender)

LEFT: Standard of 2nd Bavarian Schweres Reiter Regiment.

RIGHT AND BELOW: Trumpet Banner of the Saxon Garde Reiter Regiment.

LEFT: Drum Banner of the
Gardes Du Corps.

RIGHT: Drum Banner of Kürassier Regiment No 2.

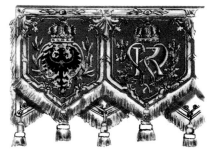

LEFT: Drum Banner of Kürassier Regiment No 4.

RIGHT: Drum Banner of Kürassier Regiment No 7.

LEFT: Drum Banner of Kürassier Regiment No 8.

RIGHT: Rear view of Mantel showing slit for use on horseback and General Officers' piping on the pockets and belt. BELOW: Red distinctions on General Officers' paletot.

Paletot

This very elegant overcoat was pale grey and had a low collar which, when folded up, reached the lobe of the ear. When folded down the collar of the coat worn beneath it clearly showed above the overcoat collar. The paletot reached to approximately nine and a half inches above the instep but photographs reveal that there was, in fact, a great deal of variety in the lengths and in the colour of the garment. The back of the paletot had a central pleat and a short horizontal half-belt with one button and two vertical pockets with scalloped flaps on either side. The coat had a slit behind the left hand side pocket (which was cut on a deep slant) through which the suspender for the undress sword was passed.

Mantel

This heavier, and much longer coat, fitted much closer at the neck and had a collar cut so deep that when turned up it covered the ears. It reached within approximately two inches of the ankles and had a deep slit at the rear which enabled the back to be spread over a horse. The back was cut and decorated as the paletot.

The coats had various methods of fastening the collar when it was turned up. The old style single breasted garment (which often had a fur collar or a hood) had two gilt lions heads and a chain. The mantel and paletot had either a small ∪ shaped piece of cloth which fastened to a button on either side of the underside of the collar, or hooks and

Regiment	Collar folded down	Collar turned up
Garde du Corps	White piped red	Red
Garde Kür Regt	Red	Dark Blue piped red
1st Regt	Dark Blue	Black velvet piped white

RIGHT: The Kaiser and Prinz zu Fürstenberg in the mantel. Note the feldbinde and the pouch belt.

Keselpauker Kürassier Regiment No 6 in Parade Dress. Note drum banner detail.

ABOVE, LEFT: Old pattern officers' mantel with pelerine. (This coat was almost ankle length). ABOVE, RIGHT: Officer in paletot over the waffenrock and wearing the undress cap. BELOW: The staff of General of Cavalry Liman von Sanders showing a variety of coats. Those officers with plumed helmets are not Kürassiers but General Staff officers.

ABOVE: An officer of the 8th
Regiment in the umhang.
Note the manöverkappe to the
helmet.

RIGHT: Officer in the umhang
and manöverkappe.

ABOVE: On the left an officer of a Line Kürassier Regiment in the mantel. Note the rear view of the paletot and the detail of the pockets and belt and difference in length.

eyes. The latter are visible on many photographs and seemed to have become more popular as the 20th century progressed. On the insides of the paletot collar, only visible when the coat was worn open, were two point-ended tabs. These were grey on one side and the collar colour on the other and were used to secure the neck when the coat was worn flung over the shoulders with the arms free. The left hand tab had a button, the right a slit and these buttoned across the throat.

Umhang (Officers' Cloak)

In 1889 a grey cloak was authorised for officers. Reaching to well below the knee the cloak could be worn alone or over the paletot. It had a fly front (buttons covered) and two inside pockets. The collar of the cloak was coloured differently when turned up and folded down in the same manner as the paletot. It could be fitted with a detachable hood for foul weather buttoned on either side under the folded down collar, or inside it.

Photographs show the cloak to have been a voluminous garment which well covered a mounted officer's knees and laid well back over the horses back behind the saddle.

RIGHT: Umhang or Officers' cloak, this could be worn over the paletot if desired.

BELOW: Insignia detail, worn on Mantel by NCOs

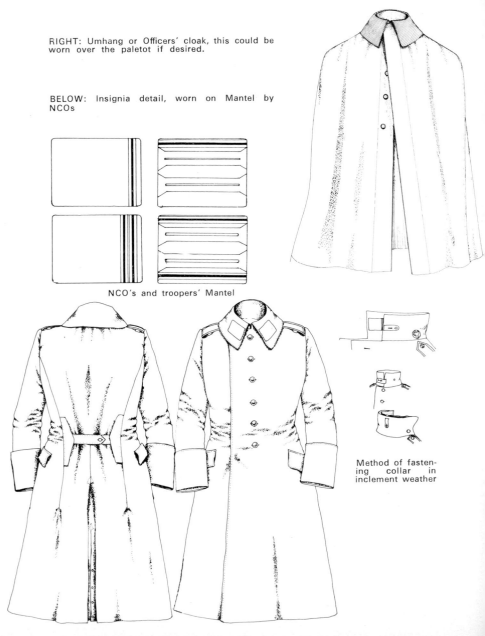

NCO's and troopers' Mantel

Method of fastening collar in inclement weather

ABOVE: A group of cavalry officers wearing the paletot, mantel, and and überrock. Note the remarkable difference in the colours of the coats, the tabs on the collar of the officer in the mantel and the undress cap of the trooper of fähnrich on the left at the rear, also his collar patches.

Mantel (Greatcoat of the NCO's and troopers)

The overcoat for non-commissioned ranks was a long, single-breasted grey coat with a deep turned down collar, and deep cuffs. It had a long slit at the rear to facilitate its use when mounted and had a short belt across the waist at the rear closed by one button. The coat had six buttons down the front and the regiments were distinguished by the shoulder straps, which were as for the undress tunic, and also by rectangular patches on the collar fronts which were in the regimental facing colour for all except the 6th Regiment which had poppy red distinctions. The Guard Regiment had two white lace bars on each patch. When on duty the sabre belt was worn over the greatcoat.

Sommerrock (Officers' Summer Tunic)

For the summer half-year, officers could wear a white single breasted undress tunic closed by eight regimental buttons down the front. The coat was cut like the dark blue undress tunic but had no coloured facings or pipings. The cuffs were plain and the shoulder cords were sewn directly to the coat without bridles or frogs.

Litewka (Officers' Working Tunic)

A blue, single breasted, working tunic was worn by the officers until 1903. Called a Litewka it was originally a Lithuanian coat worn as part of the male national costume of that country. This tunic was fly fronted with plain cuffs, a folded down collar (hooked close in front), two horizontal pockets with rectangular flaps in the sides of the skirts and a further single pocket set in the left breast.

A new, light grey pattern, was introduced in 1903. This tunic was double breasted and had two rows of six buttons, deep round cuffs, a looser, stand and fall, collar (with oblong collar tabs) and a horizontal

BELOW: Old pattern litewka being worn by the NCO on right. Men in background are in stable dress with mütze.

Officers' Litewka

pocket on each side of the skirt. The fronts and lower edge of the collar, the edge of the front and around the cuffs were piped in colour. The collar tabs were white and were also piped and had a button on each. The shoulder cords were worn on this coat.

Regiment	Patch	Piping	Buttons
Garde du Corps	White	Red	Silver
Garde Kür Regt	White (piped blue)	Red	Silver
1st Regt	White (piped black velvet)	White	Gold
2nd Regt	White	Red	Silver
3rd Regt	White	Light Blue	Silver
4th Regt	White	Red	Silver
5th Regt	White	Red	Gold
6th Regt	White	Blue	Gold
7th Regt	White	Yellow	Silver
8th Regt	White (piped green)	White	Gold

Litewka (NCO's and Troopers' Working Tunic)

For the NCO's and troopers' the Litewka was a single breasted garment with a fly front. The collar was turned down and had patches in the regimental facing colour, red for the 6th Regiment. NCO's had rank strips on these patches and NCO's lace on the fronts and lower edge of the collar.

The Wachtmeister had, in addition, a chevron ornament worn on the left upper sleeve.

Drillisachen (Fatigue and Stable Dress)

For fatigue duty in the barracks, drills and for mucking out stables, etc, the rank and file wore a loose greyish-yellow drill, short coat with a low standing collar and six small horn buttons down the front. NCO's wore a narrow white, black striped braid band along the top and front edge of the collar, troopers a small cord of the province colours along the bottom of the collar and the One Year Volunteer a cord on the left shoulder

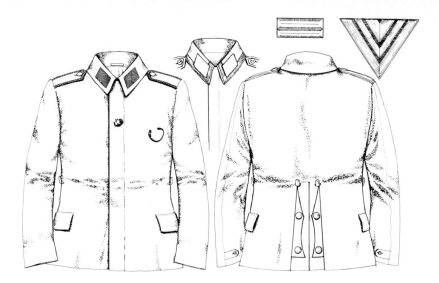

Litewka for NCO's and troopers with, inset, NCO's collar lace, rank strips and arm chevrons of the Wachtmeister

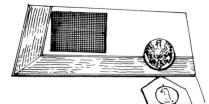

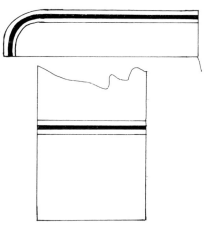

ABOVE: Litewka of Sergeant showing lacing, patch in facing colour and NCO's button. RIGHT: Drillisach collar of NCO's and braid stripe of Etats-mässige Wachtmeister

also in the province colours. The Etatsmässige Wachtmeister had an additional strip of braid around the sleeve at approximately cuff depth.

Reithosen (Riding Breeches and Boots)

The riding breeches of the cuirassiers were white kirsey reinforced inside the legs and over the seat with white leather. At the turn of the century two types of boots were still in use. The old 'Brandenburg' type which came only up to the knee with a very deep belled cuff, and the 1888 model jackboot which had a much stiffer leg part and came up over the knee at the front and cut below the knee at the rear. The old Brandenburg type were rapidly dispensed with. The boots had buckled on nickelled spurs, silver for the officers, kept up by a projecting step in the heel.

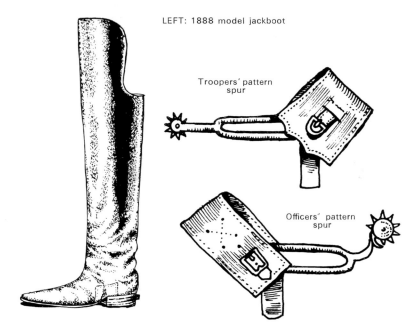

LEFT: 1888 model jackboot

Troopers' pattern spur

Officers' pattern spur

Langetuchhosen (Long trousers)

For walking out and undress duties very dark blue black trousers were worn. These trousers were worn during the winter months of the year and were suported on wide canvas braces. They had poppy red stripes down the outside of each leg except in the case of the 2nd Regiment which had crimson, and the 5th which had rose red piping. Photographs suggest that the officers' trousers were cut narrower than those of the NCO's and troopers and that they were strapped under the shoe. Officers also wore the dark blue trousers for some mounted duties. Light boots with buckled on spurs were worn under the trousers. During the hot weather season wide white linen trousers were worn. For gala wear officers affected special white trousers with a stripe of the full dress tunic braid down each outside leg. With these trousers special boots which had a foot like the riding boot but a close fitting leg part of light quality white leather were worn.

Stulphandschuhe (Gauntlets)

These were worn with the full dress tunic and with riding breeches. Photographs reveal that for officers at least these gloves were, in fact, the short hand glove but with a separate cuff, through which the 'tail' of the cuff protruded. With the red gala waffenrock the Gardes du Corps and the Guard Regiment wore short white wash leather gloves.

Feldbinde (Officers' Undress waist belts)

These belts were for orders of dress when the sash was not worn. The belts were approximately 5 cm wide and were made in silver woven thread with silk stripes worked in. In the case of Prussian cuirassier regiments the silk stripes were black. The belts were closed by the

circular locket and clasp type buckle in the button colour and had a vertical slide on either side of this. The locket design for Prussian Regiments was the cypher 'WR II' with a crown over, the clasps encircled in a closed wreath of laurel.

Brustschilder (Gorgets)

On July 4, 1895, on the anniversary of the Battle of Hohenfriedberg the Kaiser authorised the issue of a regimental gorget to all ranks of the 2nd Regiment. For the troopers the gorget and its chain were highly polished brass with a central 'German Silver' ornament (a matt finished cartouche bearing the 'line' eagle surrounded by a trophy of twenty flags and four cannon barrels surmounted by the crown and with a baroque plate beneath inscribed '1745'). The NCO's gorget was nickelled and its central ornament and rim were all brass. The Officers' pattern was a silver/gilt gorget with a gilded rim and chain, the central ornament silvered and gilded, the cartouche red enamelled, the eagle black and gold, the oak leaves green and gold and the flags silver. The shield and chain were lined with crimson cloth.

The following year on January 27, 1896 the 1st Regiment were also awarded a gorget as a regimental distinction. In this case the troopers' pattern was in nickelled silver with supporting chains in similar metal. The central ornaments on the troopers' gorgets were brass. The NCO's gorget was also nickelled silver but with the centre in silvered

RIGHT: Kronprinz Wilhelm in the uniform of an officer of Kürassier Regiment No 2 wearing the waffenrock with helmet. He wears the gorget issued to the 2nd Regiment in 1895.

ABOVE, TOP: Gorget pattern for Leib Kürassier Regiment. ABOVE, BOTTOM: Gorget pattern Kürassier Regiment No 2. ABOVE, RIGHT: Officer of Kürassier Regiment No 2 in waffenrock with epaulettes and gorget. RIGHT: Officer of Kürassier Regiment No 1 in waffenrock with gorget. Note that these officers are wearing epaulettes with the waffenrock.

metal, with a black enamelled eagle. The officers' pattern was plated silver but had a gilded central trophy, a gilt rim and a gilt support chain on black velvet. The ornament comprised a circular centre bearing the Old Prussian Eagle (flying from the earth to the sun with a crown and motto scroll above it) and a shell shaped baroque cartouche beneath it bearing the 'W II' cypher, and cn either side, '1674' and '1896'. On either side of the central circle were trophies of armour backed by four flags, two pikes and two cannon. For officers the central circlet was silver, the eagle black and gold, the sun gold, the motto scroll red and gold, the earth green and the sky light blue. When the cuirass was worn a similar device was carried on its breast part. For the 1st Regiment this comprised the central motif from the gorget and for the 2nd a small version of the entire gorget. Gorgets of the officers of the 1st Regiment were lined with black velvet. The Musikmeisters wore the NCO's pattern. The gorget was worn both with the full dress and undress tunics.

Kartusche-Bandolier (Pouch Belt)
For NCO's and troopers the belt was thick whitened leather with brass mountings. The officers had facing colour cloth belts faced with

A

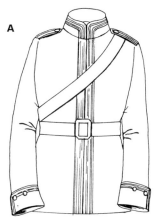

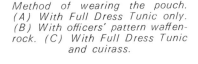

Method of wearing the pouch. (A) With Full Dress Tunic only. (B) With officers' pattern waffenrock. (C) With Full Dress Tunic and cuirass.

C

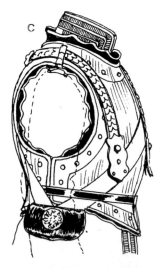

B

ABOVE: Rear view of an officer of a line regiment showing small pouch with cypher plate. LEFT, TOP TO BOTTOM: Pouch lid patterns; 1st Regiment; 2nd Regiment; 3rd to 8th Regiments

Officers' pouch lid ornamentation

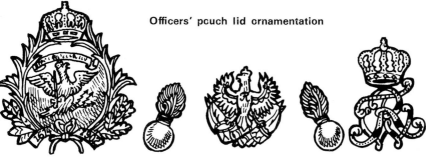

1st Regiment   2nd Regiment   3rd to 8th Regiments

ribbed gold or silver lace according to the button colour and with a corded edging in the facing colour.

Kartusche Kasten (The Pouch)

For the NCO's and troopers of all regiments the pouch was made of polished black leather. On the flap was an ornament which differed from regiment to regiment.

The Guard Regiment had the brass Guard Star. The 1st Regiment an oval brass plate impressed with the Old Brandenburg Eagle with a motto scroll above surrounded with a wreath of palm and with 1674 and 1902 beneath. NCO's and troopers of the 2nd Regiment had a circular plate impressed with the Prussian Line Eagle on a trophy of cannon drums and flags with a large brass grenade on either side. All other regiments had a circular plate with the Line Eagle and trophy.

Officers had a smaller pouch, the Guard Regiment had a Silver Star plate, the 1st Regiment a gilded ornament comprising the Brandenburg Eagle with a crown above surrounded with palm sprays and with 1674 and 1902 beneath, and the 2nd Regiment the Line Eagle on its trophy only (circular brass plate omitted) and with two smaller gilded grenades. Officers of the remaining regiments wore the 'FWR' cypher and crown in gilt on the pouch lid.

Offiziere Schärpe (Officers' Sash)

For full dress a woven silver sash was worn around the waist, retained on the left hip by a slide with tassels descending to knee level. The sash had two stripes in the province colour and netted knots above the tassels.

RIGHT: Officers' sash pattern. Centre two stripes are in province colour. LEFT: Figure showing how the sash was worn with the cuirass

'Schabraken/Schabrunken' (Housings and Wallet Flaps)

The cuirassier horse furniture comprised a housing and wallet flaps. The housing was a rectangular piece of the facing cloth carried under the saddle and the wallet flaps were hexagonal covers of the facing cloth carried over the brown leather wallets. The points of the hexagonal flaps were at the bottom, the officers' pattern had slightly splayed sides and a rounded base. Both the housing and the wallet flaps were in the regimental facing colour except for the 6th Regiment which had poppy red. Both items were edged with a double band of worsted cloth in the button colour, the two strips separated by a 'light' of the facing colour. The outer band was narrower than the inner. The officers' housings and wallets had silver or gold lace bands and had a similar central 'light'.

GARDE KÜRASSIER REGIMENT

The 'light' between the edging bands was red and both the housing and the wallet flaps were decorated with Guard Stars surmounted by crowns. The stars were white (silver for officers) and the crown yellow (gold for officers).

ABOVE: The Leib-Kürassier Regiment with special parade housing and wallet flaps.

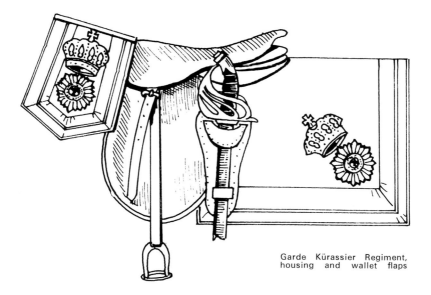

Garde Kürassier Regiment,
housing and wallet flaps

LEIB KÜRASSIER REGIMENT NO 1

From 1903 special housings and wallet flaps were worn by this regiment .The trimming was similar to the full dress tunic braid, and the ornaments, on both the housing and the flaps consisted of the Old Prussian Eagle on a white ground surrounded by a yellow baroque scroll and with a red motto band lettered 'PRO GLORIA ET PATRIA' in black and with a crown in full colours overall. For officers these ornaments and the edging bands were in rich gold lace and embroidery with coloured silk embroidery where appropriate.

Dienstdecke (The undress horse cloth)
A rectangular blue cloth worn under the saddle.

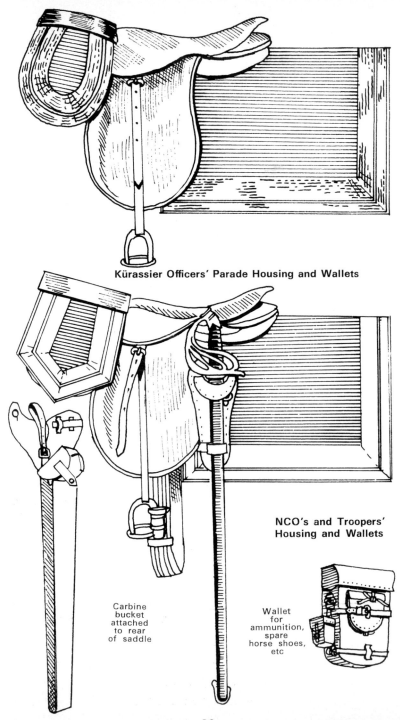

Kürassier Officers' Parade Housing and Wallets

NCO's and Troopers' Housing and Wallets

Carbine bucket attached to rear of saddle

Wallet for ammunition, spare horse shoes, etc

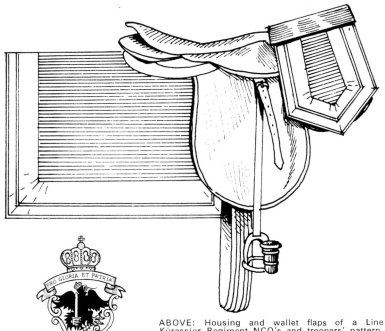

ABOVE: Housing and wallet flaps of a Line
Kürassier Regiment NCO's and troopers' pattern.
LEFT: Detail of ornaments carried on the housings and wallets of the 1st Leib Kürassier Regiment

Reitzeug/Sattel (Bridle and Saddlery)

The heavy cavalry bridle was polished brown leather with polished steel buckles, tongues, rings, etc. The bit differed from the British universal pattern in having a thicker bridoon and had a considerably lower port and shorter cheek. A throat lash was included instead of a chain and the halter rein was usually coiled and looped to the lower part of it. The boss of the bit was circular, and was decorated with the Royal cypher.

The officers' bit differed from that of the men in that the bridoon was omitted. The ends of the officers' straps were decorated with large silvered tips and their buckles were larger and octagonal.

The saddle was lighter than the British pattern, higher in the arch and with deeper and wider flaps. The girth protector flaps were made of numnah and the panels were of the same material. A thick woollen blanket 7 foot 7 inches x 6 foot 4 inches was carried folded under the saddle.

The stirrups were wider and heavier than the British counterpart and the girth was white and in the Cape or Colonial fashion. A surcingle was used.*

The wallets were large and capacious, the nearside one contained cartridges and could have a shoe case strapped to the outside. A spade or hatchet could also be attached.

A short piece of rope with a ring at one end was carried over the carbine bucket. When a number of these ropes were joined together

---

*Handbook of the German Army 1912

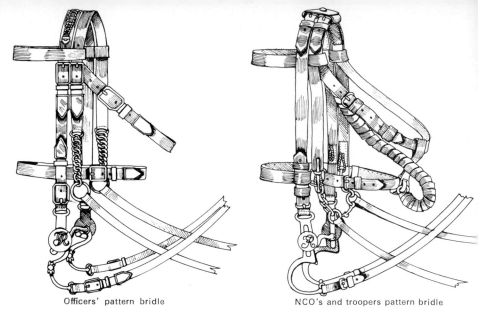

Officers' pattern bridle   NCO's and troopers pattern bridle

a large picketing rope was fashioned which was passed over two long picket staves which were usually carried in the regimental baggage.

A corn sack shaped like a sausage was strapped over the rear of the saddle and over the rolled overcoat.

A mess tin of aluminium holding approximately four and a half pints was carried in a leather case on the near side of the saddle. The tin

BELOW: Officers of a Line Kürassier Regiment in the waffenrock. Note the sabre patterns and the adjutant, immediately behind the first rider, wearing the special sash of his appointment.

ABOVE: A group of Kürassier officers in the waffenrock. Note the several different styles of Staff and Dragoon helmets clearly shown in the background. Also of interest is the horse furniture detail on the nearest horses. BELOW: Officer using the undress horse cloth.

ABOVE, LEFT AND RIGHT: Detail views of officers' pattern bridlery. Note the gorget being worn with the waffenrock, the sabre frog fastening, and the trumpeters, denoted by their shoulder wings.

cover could be used for a drinking utensil or as a frying pan and had a separate handle folded inside.

The full weight carried by a troop horse in the field was approximately 100 lb.

'Pallasch' (Sabre)

From 1876 NCO's and troopers of all cuirassier regiments carried captured French Carabinier swords. These weapons were known as the 'M 1854' pattern and had a four bar brass guard with a black leather grip (bound with brass wire) and an iron scabbard which was browned from 1905.

From 1880 the officers were also ordered to carry this type of weapon but in their case the grips were covered with black shark skin and bound with gold wire. The sword originally had a blade 97·5 cm long and 3·5 cm wide but in 1896 they were gradually modified to a length of 82·5 cm and thereafter the design of the scabbard altered so that it had only one ring.

Officers of the Guard had a small silver Guard Star welded on the sides of the grip from 1889.

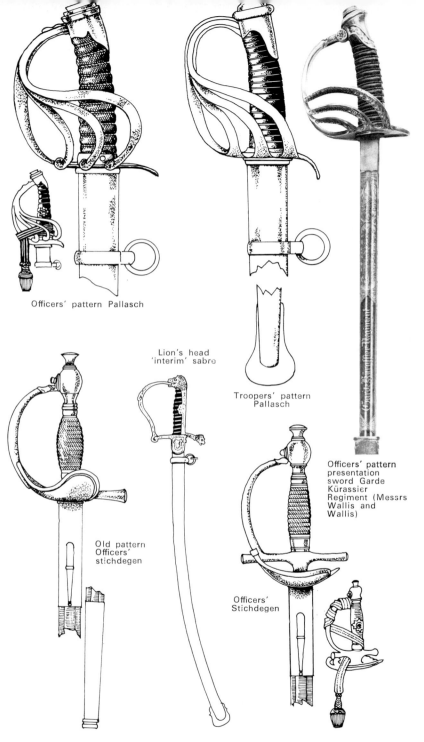

Officers' pattern Pallasch

Lion's head 'interim' sabre

Troopers' pattern Pallasch

Old pattern Officers' stichdegen

Officers' pattern presentation sword Garde Kürassier Regiment (Messrs Wallis and Wallis)

Officers' Stichdegen

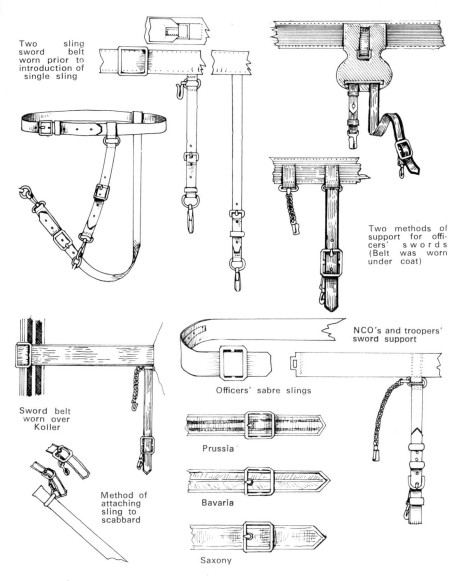

Two sling sword belt worn prior to introduction of single sling

Two methods of support for officers' swords (Belt was worn under coat)

Sword belt worn over Koller

Method of attaching sling to scabbard

NCO's and troopers' sword support

Officers' sabre slings

Prussia

Bavaria

Saxony

Stichdegen (Undress Sword)

This weapon, the so-called interim sword was carried by the officer for undress and on social occasions when the sword was ordered to be worn. The guard was the single knuckle bow type with a silver wire grip and a ball pommel. The scabbard was black leather and had a gilded 'chape'. Officers of the Guard Regiment had a small silver Guard Star welded on the sides of the grip from 1889.

Koppel (Belt)

The wide thick white leather sword belt was worn over the koller and the waffenrock by NCO's and troopers. Officers wore sword belts faced with button colour lace and edged with a piping in the facing cloth. The belt had one sling strap with a clip-hook which fastened to the ring and a short chain and clip-hook to enable the sword to be caught up.

Faustriemen/Portepee (Sword knots)
The sword knot contributed a significant detail to the German uniform and was designed to give a great deal of information concerning the rank and squadron identity of the wearer.

Each knot can be described as comprising (a) strap (b) slide (c) crown and (d) tassel.

Squadron	Strap	Slide		Crown	Tassel
1st	Red-Brown Leather	Plaited	Leather	White	White
2nd	Red-Brown Leather	Plaited	Leather	Red	White
3rd	Red-Brown Leather	Plaited	Leather	Yellow	White
4th	Red-Brown Leather	Plaited	Leather	Light-Blue	White
5th	Red-Brown Leather	Plaited	Leather	Green	White

Unteroffiziere and Sergeants
The strap and slide was in red-brown leather, the crown in white wool mixed with black for Prussian Regiments with a white tassel; a light blue and white crown and a white tassel (with a blue core) for Bavarians; white and green crown and white tassel with a green core for Saxons.

BELOW: Several different types of officers' sword knots.

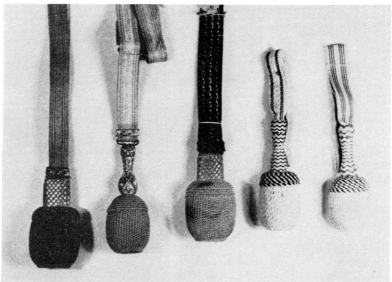

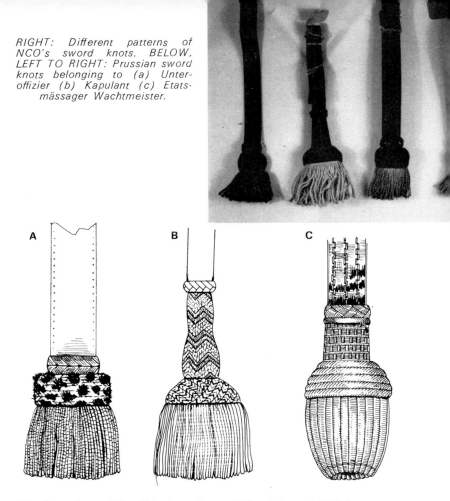

RIGHT: Different patterns of NCO's sword knots. BELOW, LEFT TO RIGHT: Prussian sword knots belonging to (a) Unteroffizier (b) Kapulant (c) Etatsmässager Wachtmeister.

A   B   C

Wachtmeister, Vize Wachtmeister, Fähnrich and Offiziere

The sword knots had a distinctive and elegant shape and were made in silver braid and cord, the straps and slides in silver and had black silk stripes worked throughout for Prussians, silver with blue for Bavarians and silver and green for Saxons. On the 'degen' the infantry pattern knot with the silver strap was carried by Prussian officers.

Kapitulant

Re-enlisted personnel carried a special honour sword knot comprising a brown leather strap and slide with the crown in the squadron colour and the tassel in a mixture of the colours of the province.

Karabiner (Carbine)

From 1888 cuirassiers carried the carbine. At first they were issued with the 1871 carbine but later the 'M98' carbine came into use along with the remainder of the German cavalry. This later weapon weighed nearly 8 lbs, had a 23 inch barrel and an overall length of approximately 3 feet 6 inches.

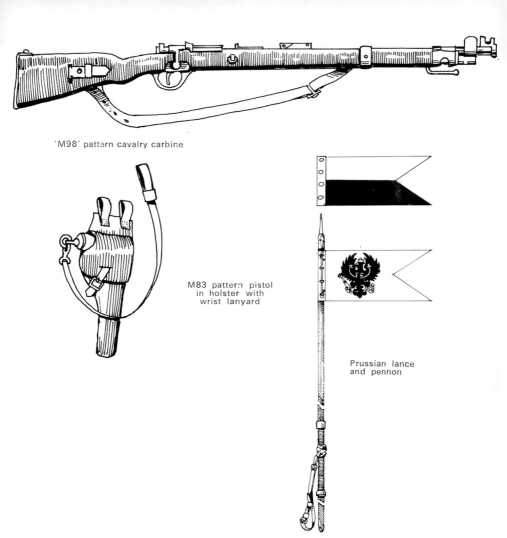

'M98' pattern cavalry carbine

M83 pattern pistol
in holster with
wrist lanyard

Prussian lance
and pennon

Pistole (Pistols)

NCO's and trumpeters carried pistols. Prussian heavy cavalry carried the 'M83' pattern pistol.

Lanze (Lance)

From 1890 the cuirassiers were armed with the M90 pattern hollow, steel shafted lance with a cruciform blade. The lance was approximately 10 feet 6 inches long and weighed some 3·94 lbs.

A brown leather strap was fixed half way down its length to loop around the troopers right arm. The grip was bound with white cord and edged at the top and bottom of the cord with two brass rings.

The Prussian lance pennon was white over black. Prussian NCO's had an entirely white pennon decorated with a black heraldic eagle.

Trompeten (Trumpets)

The signal instrument of the cavalry was the trumpet. The traditional instrument was the fanfare trumpet first introduced in the 18th century. It was a long brass trumpet with a double bend and was engraved around the bell with baroque decorations. After 1817 a shorter model was taken into use which, with few modifications, continued in use until 1914. The instrument had one bend and was approximately half

HEAD OF PAGE: Dismounted band of the 8th Kürassier Regiment in full dress tunics. Note the distinctive shoulder wings and sabres.
LEFT: Trumpeter of a Line Kürassier Regiment in full dress tunic with the late pattern trumpet carried from 1817.

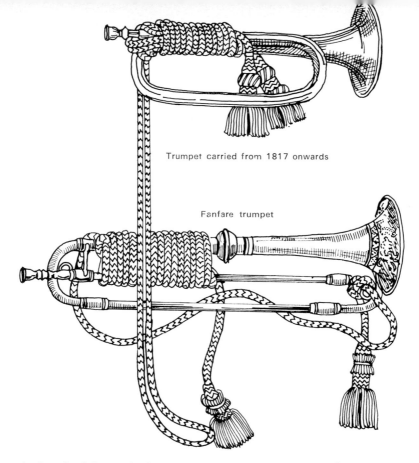

Trumpet carried from 1817 onwards

Fanfare trumpet

the length of the old fanfarentrompete. An order of December 1895 stated that the trumpet was to be 42 cm long.

The normal trumpet cords were province colour and white wool with large NCO pattern tassels, gold or silver cords being used by some regiments on parade. The Trumpet Major had silver and province colour cords.

If the old fanfare trumpet was carried on parade it had special netted cords with four additional tassels hanging from length of the double bend. The 1st regiment had silver trumpets from 1721.

PAUKEN (KETTLEDRUMS)

All cuirassier regiments had kettledrums. Given below is a table showing the various dates for the awarding of the drums to each regiment and in some cases the source of the drums.

Regiment	Date of award of drums	Metal	Notes
Garde Kürassier Regiment	1822	Silver	
1st Regiment	1718	Silver	

2nd Regiment	1820	Silver	
3rd Regiment	1758	Silver	Russian drums captured at Zorndorf.
4th Regiment	1822	Silver	
5th Regiment	1820	Silver	Drums of the former Katte-Dragoner Regiment No 4
6th Regiment	1810	Silver	Drums of the former Regiment Gendarmes (K Regt No 10)
7th Regiment	1818	Silver	Drums of the former Leib Regiment No 2
8th Regiment	1827	Silver	Also possessed two pairs of copper drums.

PAUKEN BEHÄNGE (KETTLEDRUM BANNERS)

Two patterns of kettledrum banners were carried by the cuirassier regiments. A parade or full dress set and the 'interim' or 'dienst' banners, perhaps better called the undress banners. The latter were universally in the colour of the regimental facings with decoration in the button colour and edged with bands as on the regimental housings and wallet flaps.

The full dress banners were very finely made in silk, damask and velvet, decorated with silver and gold embroidery and tassels. Information on all these banners is now difficult to trace. Some have ended in private collections while other examples are in various Museums. The illustrations have been collated from several German sources.

Unlike British kettledrum banners of the period which were generally a fine cloth or velvet strip of cloth draped around the drums and embellished with the regimental badge and battle honours the German banners were usually made in panels, either rounded or oval and in two layers with tassels attached to the bottom edges in some cases.

STANDARTEN (STANDARDS)

All cuirassier regiments carried standards to which were attached the various commemorative streamers signifying their service to the Fatherland. The following is a brief description of the standards and their streamers all of which are illustrated in colour.

THE COMMEMORATIVE CAMPAIGN STREAMERS

1813-1815 Campaign	Orange with a thin white and black stripe on either side.
1848-1849 Campaign	Black with a white stripe on either edge. This streamer was awarded with or without golden swords.
1864 Campaign	Black with an orange stripe on one edge and a white stripe on the other. Awarded with or without golden swords.
1866 Campaign	Black with white and orange stripes along each edge. Crossed swords in gilt at the bottom

ABOVE: Recruit being sworn in on the regimental standard. Note Adjutants' sash, standard bandolier and streamers on standard.

for almost all regiments taking part in the campaign.

1870-1871 Campaign

The black and white ribbon of the Iron Cross with the addition of a red central stripe. This streamer was decorated with gold clasps inscribed with the names of the various actions in which the regiment had been engaged.

1900 Parade Streamer

Awarded by the Kaiser to all regiments, this streamer was silver with three black stripes for all Prussian Regiments but half white and half blue for the Bavarians. The streamer had two gilt clasps attached to it, one with the Imperial Crown and the date '1 Januar 1900' on the reverse and the other the monogram 'WII' and the Royal Crown on the face and on the reverse two dates—'1 Januar 1900' and below it the foundation date of the regiment. For Bavaria the monogram 'LPR' replaced 'WII' and the date '18 Januar 1871' replaced '1 Januar 1900'.

Clasps awarded to commemorate the Silver Jubilee of Wilhelm II's reign in 1913 (for the Gardes du Corps, Garde Kürassier and 1st Leib Regiment only)

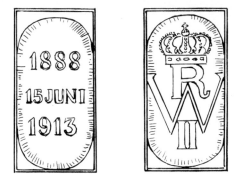

Gardes du Corps

Originally the regiment carried a standard awarded in 1741, of the old Roman 'vexillum' form. This was replaced by a new square standard in 1798 and carried until 1889. It was white damask with silver fringes and embroidery. A new standard was presented in 1890, once more in the old 'vexillum' form and again white with fringes and embroidery mainly in silver. The standard was decorated with streamers commemorating the compaigns of 1813-15, 1866 (with swords), 1870-71, the 1870 Iron Cross Streamer (awarded to regiments which already had the ornamental point of the standard haft decorated with the Iron Cross for services rendered in the 1813-15 War of Freedom against Napoleon), the 1900 commemorative streamer with additional silver clasps awarded by Kaiser Wilhelm II to his Guard regiments to mark the Silver Jubilee of his reign on June 15, 1913, a centennial streamer commemorating over one hundred years of existence, the Grand Cross star and badge of the Order of the Black Eagle on the broad orange sash of the order (awarded 8/9/1901), plus the chain and badge of the Hohenzollern House Order (awarded on June 13, 1913).

Garde Kürassier Regiment

A square standard, presented in 1891, in white with a cornflower blue centre field and corner medallions and with silver fringes and gold and silver embroidery. The standard was decorated with the streamers for 1813-1815, 1866, 1870-1871 and 1900.

Leib-Kürassier Regiment No 1

The regiment had two standards. The first of which was the Life Standard (awarded in 1896) and the Regimental Standard (presented in 1906). The former was square and of white damask with a crimson silk centre field and corner medallions and gold embroidery. It carried the 1813-1815, 1866, 1870-1871 and 1870 Iron Cross streamers plus the centennial streamer and cravat for 200 years service and the black and silver streamer with 1900 clasp and the Wilhelm II Silver Jubilee clasps.

The Regimental Standard was also square and of crimson damask with a white centre field and corner medallions and gold fringes and embroidery. This standard also bore a double centennial streamer for over 200 years existence and the streamers as for the Life Standard.

Kürassier Regiment No 2

This regiment had a swallow tailed standard of the dragoon pattern presented in 1900. It was white damask with a black centre field and gold fringing and embroidery. It was decorated with the streamers for 1813-1815, 1849 with swords, 1866, 1870-1871, 1870 Iron Cross, 1900 with clasps and centennial streamer for over 100 years existence.

Kürassier Regiment No 3

This regiment's standard was also of the dragoon swallow tailed pattern and was awarded in 1890. It was light violet with crimson corner wedges, gold fringing and was embroidered in gold. It bore the streamers for the 1813-1815 1866, 1870-1871, 1870 Iron Cross, 1900 clasps and a centennial streamer for over 100 years existence.

Kürassier Regiment No 4

This regiment had the swallow tailed pattern. The standard was presented in 1899 and was dark blue damask with golden corner wedges, gold fringes and embroidery. The standard was decorated with the streamers of 1813-1915, 1849 with swords, 1864, 1866, 1870-1871, 1870 Iron Cross, 1900 clasps and a centennial streamer for over 100 years existence.

Kürassier Regiment No 5

This regiment's standard was presented in 1901 and was also of the swallow tailed variety. The standard was black damask with scarlet corner wedges and gold embroidery and fringing. It bore the streamers for 1813-1815, 1866, 1870-1871, 1870 Iron Cross, 1900 clasps and a centennial streamer for over 100 years existence.

Kürassier Regiment No 6

This distinguished and fashionable regiment had a square standard of golden damask with fringing and embroidery in gold. It was presented

Front and rear of one of the clasps awarded with the 1900 streamer

Front and rear of the second clasp awarded with the 1900 streamer

in 1899. The standard was extensively decorated with the streamers for 1813-1815, 1864 with swords, 1866, 1870-1871, 1870 Iron Cross, 1900 clasps, double centennial streamer for over 200 years of existence and also had two very special 'parade' streamers. The first was presented on 11.6.1823 by the Grand Duchess Alexandra Feodorovna of Russia; born Princess Charlotte of Prussia. This streamer was dark blue heavily embroidered in gold with an oak leaf motif. The second, presented on 12.5.1876 by the Czar Alexander II of Russia was in the orange and black stripes of the Russian Order of St George with gold clasps and silver fringing.

Kürassier Regiment No 7

The 7th had a white square standard of white damask with crimson centre field and silver corner medallions with gold fringing and embroidery. The standard was replaced in 1903 by a second pattern of black damask with a white centre field and with black corner medallions, all the embroidery and fringing being gold. The regiment carried the streamers for 1813-1815, 1866, 1870-1871 and 1900 with clasps.

Kürassier Regiment No 8

This regiment had a very similar standard to the 5th Regiment being black with scarlet corner medallions and with gold embroidery and fringing. It had the streamers for 1813-1815, 1849 with swords, 1866, 1870-1871 and 1900 clasps.

LEFT: A Line Kürassier Regiment wearing the field grey Koller introduced to replace the old white full dress tunic for field duties shortly before World War I.

2: Bavarian Heavy Cavalry

UNTIL 1879 the Bavarian heavy cavalry comprised a Gardes du Corps and the 1st and 2nd Kürassier Regiments. From that date the character of the heavy cavalry was completely changed and thereafter they were known as Schwere Reiter or Heavy Cavalry.

Both Bavarian Heavy Cavalry were in the 'I Königliches Bayerischen Armee Korps'/1st Cavalry Division/ with Headquarters in München.

Regiment	Raised	Garrison
Königliches Bayerisches Schweres Reiter Regiment Carl von Bayern No 1	1814	München
Königliches Bayerisches Schweres Reiter Regiment Erzherzog Franz Ferdinand von Österreich-Este No 2	1815	Landshut

Basically the uniform changed little between the major alteration from cuirassier to heavy cavalry in 1879. It was in the style of the Prussian dragoon with light blue tunics (Waffenrock) and poppy red facings, the 1st Regiment having white buttons and the second yellow.

RANK DISTINCTIONS

These followed the pattern prescribed for the Prussian Cuirassiers except that the officers' shoulder cords had light blue interwoven silk 'darts' instead of the Prussian black and the epaulettes silver edging and silver or gold crescents silver bridles also with light blue stripes.

The NCO's distinctive flat metal lace on the collar and cuffs was in the button colour as were the heraldic buttons on the sides of the collars.

Trumpeters wings were poppy red decorated with gold or silver lace and the 'Stabstrompeter' and 'Musikmeister' distinctions followed the same pattern as the Prussians.

The 'Standartenträger' wore an arm badge and gorget similar to his Prussian counterpart. The pale blue arm badge carried pale blue and white Bavarian standards with the Royal Crown above the letter 'L' beneath. The gorget was also similar to the Prussian model but carried the Bavarian flags, crown and 'L'. The standard bandolier was red leather faced with light blue velvet and decorated with three bands of gold or silver lace according to the regiment, these stripes were set on so that there was a stripe of lace along each and one down the middle. Across the bandolier at the level of the third tunic button was a metal clasp.

Swordmanship chevrons, one-year volunteer, kapitulant and the telegraph school badges were in pale blue and white and in the latter case there was an additional strip of braid down the centre of the shoulder strap.

RIGHT: Typical classes of Fechtabzeichen worn on the right upper sleeve

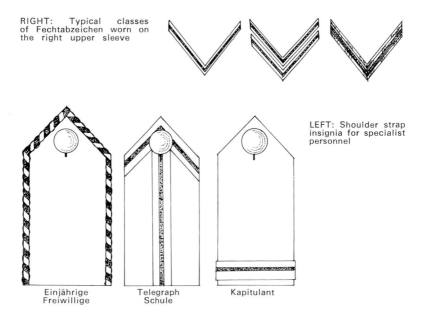

LEFT: Shoulder strap insignia for specialist personnel

Einjährige   Telegraph   Kapitulant
Freiwillige   Schule

UNIFORM AND ACCOUTREMENTS
Helme (Helmets)

A black polished leather, metal spiked, helmet (pickelhaube) with a square cut front visor, the mountings in the button colour, German silver for the 1st Regiment and brass for the 2nd. Officers' helmets mounted in silvered or gilded metal. The helmet spike had a cross form base to its column and the spikes of the officers' helmets were taller and fluted in the same style as the Prussian Regiments. For parades and certain other ceremonial occasions helmets were decorated with white horsehair plumes.

The helmet plate was the Bavarian coat of arms (comprising the oval shield; having in its centre the smaller shield and decorated with the lozenge 'bends', and the quartering with lions, supported by two lions crowned, rampant and with two tails each and their heads turned to look away from the Bavarian crown set overall). Beneath the oval shield a three section motto scroll inscribed 'In/Treue/Fest'. The plate was in German silver (silvered for officers with an enamelled centre in pale blue, black, red and white) or in brass (gilded for officers). The chin scales (each plate in ᙮ form) were suspended from circular bosses above each gap between the front and rear visors and were backed by cockades. On the right side the red white and black

RIGHT: Three variants of the Bavarian helmet plate.

Reichkokarde and on the left the Bavarian cockade which was light blue and white. The officers' cockades better detailed than those of the NCO's and troopers, deeply etched and in coloured enamel.

Mütze (Undress Cap)

In a similar pattern to the caps worn by Prussian Regiments. The cap was pale blue with a poppy red band and piping around the upper part. The Bavarian blue and white cockade appeared on the front of the lower band and the Reichkokarde, on the front of the upper part. Officers' caps were higher and had a stiffer form than those of the NCO's and troopers. The officers and the senior NCO's had a small gutta percha or leather visor to the cap.

Waffenrock (Full Dress Tunic)

A single breasted tunic with a standing, round fronted collar and Swedish cuffs. The tunics of both regiments were light blue with poppy red facings. The coat had eight flat buttons of the regimental colour down the front, two on each cuff and two on the shoulder straps with the squadron number stamped on them. The back of the coat was slit to the waist and had two vertical pockets, one on either side. The pockets were each decorated with two buttons with two further specially designed buttons at waist level to support the waist belt. The shoulder straps were poppy red and there was a red piping down the leading edge of the coat and along the edges of the pocket flaps.

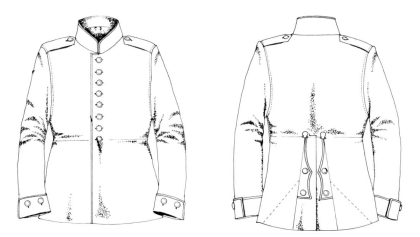
Bavarian cavalry pattern waffenrock

Überrock (The Officers' Frock)

A pale blue coat with a poppy red collar, breast linings and similar piping around the cuffs and on the pocket flaps in the rear skirts. Unlike the Prussian frock coat the Bavarian officers' frock had *seven* buttons in two rows down the double breasted front. Buttons were gilded or silvered according to the regiment.

Litewka (The Working Tunic)

The officers' pattern was rather similar to the pre-1900 Prussian litewka but in light blue cloth with a folded down and hooked close collar (without tabs or piping), single breasted with six horn buttons and two breast and skirt pockets set in the coat with scalloped flaps. The working tunic for the NCO's and troopers was grey with bright red collar patches and bright red shoulder straps.

'Mantel/Paletot/Umhang' (Officers' Greatcoats and Cloak)

The officers wore light grey, double breasted, overcoats in the Prussian style with similar differences in style between the paletot and the mantel. The collar was light blue when turned down and a bright red when turned up. The cloak also followed the Prussian pattern with similar collar detail.

The Fähnrich wore the officers' pattern greatcoat but with the same shoulder straps as the NCO's.

Mantel (Greatcoat for NCO's and Troopers)

The greatcoat followed the Prussian pattern with buttons according to the regiment. The shoulder straps and collar patches were bright red.

Drillisachen (Fatigue and Stable Dress)

The Bavarian drill coat was the same pattern as that worn by the Prussians except that the braiding was light blue and white where applicable.

Reithose (Riding Breeches)

Blue black, the officers' pattern almost black. No piping down the outside of the legs but leather strapping on the insides of the legs and across the seat for the rank and file.

Langetuchsterhosen (Long Trousers)

Light blue trousers with a 5 cm wide red stripe down the outside seams were worn for walking out and social occasions. In summer, wide, white linen, trousers were worn, narrower and better cut for the officers, strapped under the instep.

Feldbinde (The Officers' Undress Waist Belt)

The Bavarians had a silver belt with two pale blue stripes. The locket and clasp were in the button coloured metal and the locket design the Bavarian Crown, the clasp encircled by an enclosed wreath of laurel.

LEFT: The Bavarian officers' undress waist belt.

Bandolier/Kartuschkasten (Pouch and pouch belt)

The officers' pouch belt was red, faced with silver lace and decorated with three light blue silk stripes and with silver mounts.

The pouch was also red, Moroccan leather, with a silver plated lid decorated with the Bavarian Arms with palm and laurel sprays beneath it.

The NCO's and troopers had white leather pouch belts with brass mounts and a black leather pouch without any plate.

RIGHT: Bavarian officers' pouch bearing the State Coat of Arms with laurel sprays beneath.

Paradeuberlegedecke (Schabraque)

The parade schabraques (worn over the saddle) for officers and the rank and file were light blue with rounded corners and a wide band of poppy red braid around the edge. In the rear corners were red Bavarian crowns. The officers undress horse cloth was a very dark blue-black plain rectangular cloth. From 1910 the full dress schabraques were no longer worn.

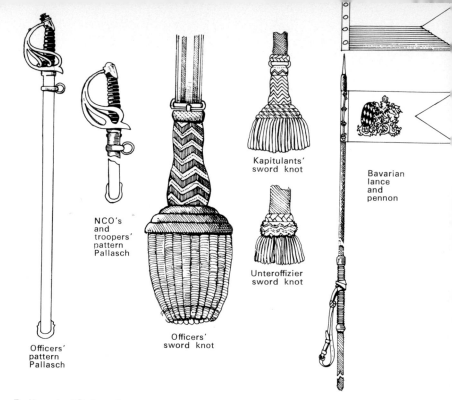

NCO's and troopers' pattern Pallasch

Kapitulants' sword knot

Bavarian lance and pennon

Unteroffizier sword knot

Officers' sword knot

Officers' pattern Pallasch

Pallasch (Sabres)

The Bavarian sword had a straight blade, brass hilt with a four bar guard and a brass backing piece to the black leather grip, which was bound with brass wire. The officers' sword followed the same pattern but the guard etc, was gilded, and the grip bound with gold wire. The scabbards were browned steel.

The officers' sword belt was red faced with silver lace which was decorated with three light blue silk stripes and with silver clasps. The belt had the short carrying strap only, no trail sling and the clip-hook for hooking the sword up. The belts of the NCO's and troopers were whitened leather with brass buckles.

Portepee/Faustriemen (Sword Knots)

The officers' sword knots were a slightly different pattern to their Prussian counterparts. The strap was silver with two light blue stripes on red Moroccan leather, the slide and the 'stalk' were light blue worked through silver cord, the crown silver cord worked with light blue velvet and the tassel silver bullion. The sword knots of the troopers followed the pattern of the Prussian cuirassiers. For the Kapitulanten the strap and slide were red-brown leather, the stalk was light blue and white, and the crown was light blue and white mixed, and the tassel was light blue and white. The NCO's had red-brown straps and slides, light blue and white crowns, and tassels with a light blue core and white outside.

Lanze (Lance)

The lance followed the Prussian pattern with an hollow steel shaft and a steel cruciform spike. The lance pennon was white over light blue, the NCO's had an all white pennon with the Bavarian golden crowned lion grasping an oval shield of pale blue and white lozenges in the centre.

PAUKEN (KETTLEDRUMS)

Both the Bavarian heavy cavalry regiments carried kettledrums. The 1st Regiment carried the silver drums of the former Bavarian Gardes du Corps.

The kettledrum banners were light blue velvet embroidered in gold or silver and had the Bavarian Arms embroidered in their true colours.

STANDARTEN (STANDARDS)

Both regiments carried standards. The 1st Regiment had theirs presented in 1815. On one side the field was light blue silk with the Bavarian State Arms in the centre and gold embroidered oak leaves in each corner. The edges were also decorated with gold embroidery all round and the flag was fringed with silver. On the reverse side the standard field carried the crowned monogram 'MJK' surrounded by gold embroidered laurel sprays and the gold oak leaves in the corners. The standard haft was painted light blue and had a gilded spear head at the tip. The haft was decorated with gold cords and tassels and carried the commemorative medals for 1815, 1866, 1870-1871, together with the Prussian streamer of the 1870-1871 campaign. The 1900 streamer and a centennial streamer also decorated the standard.

The 2nd Regiment had a standard which was awarded in 1819. It was similar to that of the 1st Regiment except that the field was white silk and all the embroidery was in silver. The haft was painted light blue. The cords and tassels were also silver and the standard had the commemorative medals for 1815, 1866, 1870-1871, the Prussian streamer 1870-1871 and the 1900 streamer.

3: Saxon Cavalry Regiments

THE Saxon cavalry comprised two heavy regiments. The premier heavy cavalry unit was the Royal Saxon Guard Cavalry Regiment (1st Heavy Regiment) which was formed from the Saxon Cuirassier Regiment in 1828 and the Royal Saxon Carabinier Regiment (2nd Heavy Regiment) raised in 1849. Both regiments had uniform characteristics of cuirassiers and carried kettledrums, but had no standards.

Title	Raised	Facings	Buttons	Garrison	Army Corps
Königliches Sächsen-Garde Reiter Regiment (1 Schweres Regiment)	1680	White	Yellow	Dresden	XII
Königliches Sächsen-Karabiner Regiment (2 Schweres Regiment)	1849	Black (Black velvet facings for officers and Senior NCO's	Yellow	Borna	XIX

SONDERABZEICHEN (TRADE AND PROFICIENCY BADGES)

Saxon cavalry wore similar trade and proficiency badges to the Prussians except that where applicable the colours were white and green and not white and black. The cockade was white and green and the Officers, NCO's and Kapitulanten sword knots were similarly coloured silver or white and green as appropriate.

Until 1905 recruits who had attended the Saxon Riding Establishment (Reitanstalt-Dresden) were distinguished by short, white/green braid strips worn on each arm above the cuff, in the case of the heavy cavalry parallel with the edge of the cuff.

After 1905 the badge for having attended the riding school was a narrow white braid as a bridle across the brass epaulettes near the crescent end, wider for two years and personnel who attended the Telegraph School had a small 'ʌ' shaped green-striped white braid across the narrower, button end of the epaulette.

ABOVE: Wilhelm Ernst, Grand Duke of Sax-Weimar in the uniform of the 2nd Saxon Cavalry Regiment (Karabiniers) (R. G. Harris Collection).

The distinguishing badge of the One-Year Volunteer was the same pattern as the Prussian cuirassiers except that it was in the provincial colours, ie, a green and white twisted cord edging to the bridles of the epaulettes and around the edge of the shoulder straps of the overcoat.

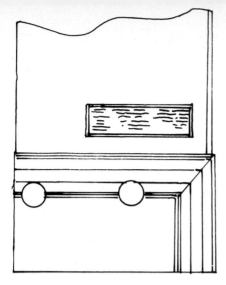

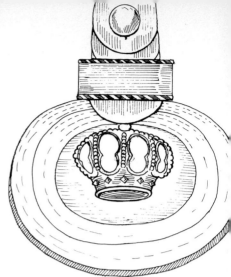

Sonderabzeichen braid strip worn on both sleeves by recruits at the Saxon Riding Establishment (Reitanstalt-Dresden)

Saxon cavalry epaulette showing Einjährige Freiwillige braid on bridle and crown device for the Guard Regiment

TROMPETER/MUSIKMEISTER
(TRUMPETER/BANDMASTER)

The principal distinction in the dress of the Saxon trumpeter was the decoration to the fronts of the koller and the absence of wings. The decoration to the fronts of the tunic comprised thirteen bars of white, point-ended bars of worsted cloth (known as 'bandlitzen') worn across the breasts of the coat, tapering from the collar to the waist, and then widening out again to the bottom of the fronts. Saxon trumpeters wore the Prussian pattern wings on the litewka.

Trumpeters of the Karabinier Regiment wore red hair plumes on the helmets for parade dress.

The Musikmeister had double the number of loops down the breast of the tunic and they were in silver lace instead of worsted cloth. The loops were very close so that hardly any of the coat was visible between them. The Musikmeister had the added distinction of wearing officers' pattern gilded epaulettes with special silver lyre badges on each.

BELOW: Trumpet Corps of the Saxon Karabinier Cavalry Regiment in Parade Uniform.

ABOVE: Trumpet Corps of the Saxon Guard Cavalry Regiment in Undress Parade Uniform. RIGHT: Kesselpauker, Saxon Guard Cavalry Regiment in Undress Parade Uniform. These are the Undress Parade copper drums with the drum banners presented to the regiment in 1872.

TRUMPET BANNERS

On the occasion of the Silver Jubilee of his reign, on April 18, 1988, King Albert of Saxony presented trumpet banners to his Guard Cavalry Regiment. They were carried on the silver fanfare trumpets which had been awarded to the regiment after the First Silesian War.

The banners had on one side, on a blue ground, the crowned monogram 'AR' surrounded by laurel branches, all embroidered in white silk and surrounded by a white and blue cord and fringes of the same colours. On the reverse side the banners had, on a yellow ground, a brown lion supporting the Crowned Arms of Saxony.

UNIFORM AND ACCOUTREMENTS

Helme (Helmets)

The helmet was same shape as the Prussian cuirassier helmet and in tombak for both regiments. It had German Silver mountings and had a helmet plate consisting of the Saxon armorial Star in German Silver (the central arms in tombak and a tombak laurel leaf wreath). The cockades were Reichkokarde and the State green and white. Officers' helmets had the mountings silvered and the front plate silvered with gilded central arms and wreath. For parades and ceremonial occasions

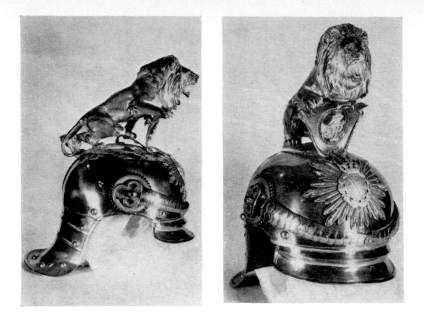

ABOVE AND BOTTOM LEFT: Officers' helmets Saxon Guard Regiment (Tradition). BOTTOM RIGHT: Troopers' pattern (Tradition).

the Guard Regiment wore, in lieu of the spike, an imposing German Silver crouching lion crest. The lion supported with its right front paw a baroque upright shield decorated with an oval cartouche with a raised and corded rim with the monogram 'FAR' and the Saxon crown. The ornament was silvered for the officers. The Karabinier Regiment wore a white hair plume for parade.

RIGHT: The central shield of the Saxon helmet plate. BELOW: NCO's of the Saxon Guard Cavalry Regiment in waffenrocks and wearing the parade lion on the helmet.

Mütze (Undress Cap)

The cap was the same pattern as the Prussian undress cap and was cornflower blue with a band in the facing colour and a white piping around the upper part. The lower band was piped with white in the case of the Karabinier Regiment whose officers also had the distinction of using black velvet for their cap bands. On the lower band the green and white Saxon cockade and on the upper part the ubiquitous Reichkokarde cockade.

Koller (Full Dress Tunic)

The coat was a similar pattern to that worn by the Prussian cuirassiers but in cornflower blue cloth for both regiments. The collars and cuffs were in the facing colour with a piping of cornflower blue. The pipings around the armholes, down the back seams and the arm seams and on the skirt pockets was white. For Saxon Cavalry Regiments these skirt pockets had a traditional 'Saxon' shape. The tunic braid was white with cornflower blue stripes for the Guard Regiment and black stripes for the Karabiniers, and gold for the officers with blue silk stripes along either edge for the Guard, and black velvet stripes for the Karabiniers. The tunics were fastened by hooks and eyes, and the bridles to retain the shoulder ornaments were cornflower blue.

The Saxon Regiments wore brass epaulettes with brass crescents, on a cornflower blue underlay. The troopers and NCO's of the Guard Regiment had brass crowns on these ornaments as regimental distinction. The flat shoulder strap part of the officers' epaulettes were decorated in a brass chain link design, those of the NCO's and troopers of 'D' shaped flat plates. The officers' epaulettes were gilded without regimental distinctions and had Saxon pattern silver rank stars. The field officers had silver fringing. The officers also had small bridles comprising gilded chain.

Shoulder cords for officers were silver with green 'darts' and lined with cornflower blue. The Guard Regiment was distinguished by gilded 'FAR' cyphers with Saxon crowns above on these cords.

BELOW: Saxon pattern officers' epaulette. RIGHT: Saxon koller with special 'Saxon' pockets.

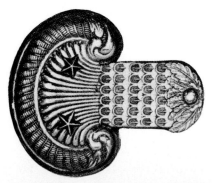

Überrock (Officers' Frock)

Pale blue with the collar in the facing colour, piped white for the Karabiniers. The pipings on the cuffs and on the pockets were white for both regiments. The coat was double breasted in the same design as the Prussian frock and had facing colour breast linings and gilded buttons for both regiments. The Fähnrich was permitted to wear this frock but with the rank and file shoulder ornaments.

Litewka (Working Tunic)

The officers wore the Prussian double breasted pattern with collar tabs in the facing colour. The Karabinier Regiment had white pipings to these tabs and both regiments had white pipings where applicable elsewhere on the coats. The NCO's and troopers wore the Prussian cuirassier pattern coat with collar patches in the facing colour and with 'Saxon' type cornflower blue shoulder straps with white pipings. Trumpeters had facing colour wings in the Prussian style on this coat.

Mantel/Paletot/Umhang (Officers' Overcoats and Cloak)

These garments all followed the Prussian pattern as described in detail under the cuirassier section. The Guard Regiment had a collar which showed cornflower blue piped white when turned down and white when turned up. The Karabinier Regiment showed the similar collar when turned down but black piped white when turned up.

Mantel (Overcoat of the NCO's and Troopers)

The overcoat was the same pattern as the Prussian garment with yellow buttons and collar patches in the regimental facing colour. The shoulder straps were the 'Saxon' type rectangular pattern (not point ended) and cornflower blue with white piping. The Guard Regiment were distinguished by yellow 'FAR' cyphers on the shoulder straps.

Saxon Cavalry overcoat shoulder strap showing device for Guard Regiment

'Drillisachen' (Fatigue and Stable Dress)

The fatigue jacket was the same pattern as worn by the Prussians except that the braiding was green and white where applicable.

Reithose/Langetuchhosen (Riding Breeches and Trousers)

The Saxon heavy cavalry had white riding breeches with leather strapping after the Prussian pattern worn with the black 'reitstiefel' but for other, dismounted, occasions and walking out, long cornflower blue trousers with white piping down the outside seams were worn.

For gala dress officers of the 1st Regiment affected cornflower blue trousers with a white stripe down the outside of the legs. The Karabiniers had similar trousers but with black stripes.

Bandolier/Kartuschekasten (Pouch and Pouch Belts)

The officers' pouch belt was cornflower blue for the Guard Regiment and black velvet for the Karabiniers both faced with silver lace. On the breast part a gilt shield shaped ornament bearing the Saxon Royal Arms surmounted by a crown and surrounded by a wreath of laurel sprays. The officers' pouches were faced with silver lace on pale blue velvet for the 1st Regiment and black velvet for the 2nd. In the centre of the lid was the Saxon shield with the crown over and surrounded with a trophy of flags cannons, etc. Around the rim of the lid was a border of linked Saxon trefoils.

For NCO's and troopers the sword belt and pouch belt were thick white leather. The sword belt fastened by a rectangular buckle on which a crown and the Saxon motto 'PROVIDENTIAE MEMOIR' appeared. The NCO's pouch was brass with a black leather lid decorated with the Saxon arms in brass surrounded by palm and laurel sprays and the troopers' pattern was plain black.

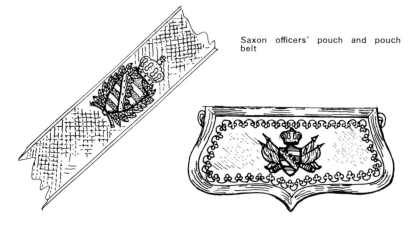

Saxon officers' pouch and pouch belt

Schärpe (The Officers' Sash)

The Saxon sash was silver with two green stripes (three for the General Officers). The sash had similar tassels to the Prussian and the Adjutants' sash also followed a similar design.

Feldbinde (The Officers' Undress Waist Belt)

The Saxons had a silver belt with two green stripes (three for the General Officers with three stripes also on the slides). The locket and clasp were in the button coloured metal, the locket with the Gothic 'FA' with a crown over and the clasp encircled by a closed wreath of laurel.

Paradeüberlegedecke (Schabraques)

A special feature of the Saxon heavy cavalry was the black sheepskin schabraques worn for parade. These sheepskin saddle covers were plain black for the NCO's and troopers but were decorated with silver, eight pointed stars in the rear corners for the officers. The stars were on pale blue backing for the Guard Regiment and on black for the Karabiniers.

The officers also had black bearskin flounces over the tops of the wallets. The wallet flaps were light blue for the Guard Regiment and black for the Karabiniers and had silver eight pointed stars in their centres. The edges of the wallet flaps were decorated with tunic braid, in the case of the Field Officers with a double row of the braid trimming.

The undress saddle cloth was dark blue.

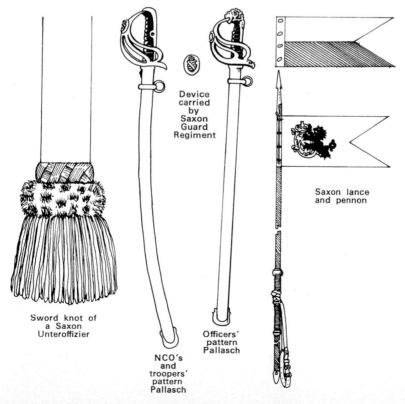

Device carried by Saxon Guard Regiment

Saxon lance and pennon

Sword knot of a Saxon Unteroffizier

Officers' pattern Pallasch

NCO's and troopers' pattern Pallasch

Pallasch (Sabres)

Cavalry sabre 'M89' with steel guard with Saxon Arms for the Karabinier Regiment and a straight bladed sword with a brass guard and with a small plate bearing the Saxon Arms on the first bar for the Saxon Guard Regiment. The swords were carried on one ring only.

Officers of both regiments carried the lion's head interim sabre of the Prussian cuirassier 1810 pattern for undress duties. From May 1913 the Karabinier Regiment officers had a silver guard to this sword.

Portepees/Faustriemen (Sword Knots)

Saxon sword knots followed the Prussian pattern except that state colours were substituted for the Prussian where appropriate. Officers' sword knots were silver and green with a black, silver decorated strap.

Lanze (Lance) and Karabiner/Revolver

The Saxon lance had a wooden shaft, steel blade and a brass ring for the arm strap. The pennon was white over green, plain white for the NCO's with a black Saxon lion grasping a golden shield with the Saxon Arms in colour surmounted by a golden crown in the centre. Prussian carbines and revolvers were carried. Some officers had ·433 Sharps revolvers.

PAUKEN (KETTLEDRUMS)

Standards were not carried but both regiments had kettle-drums. From 1872 the Guard Regiment carried the silver drums previously carried by the 'Roell/Holstein' Dragoner Regt. The banners were light blue with light blue rosettes and silver embroidered ornaments, fringing and tassels. On the panels was the cypher 'JR' with golden crowns. For undress parades copper drums were carried.

The Karabinier Regiment carried drums awarded in 1905 by the Grand Duke William Ernest of Saxon Weimer Eisenach.

The upper panels were cornflower blue; lower panels black. The five upper panels showed different emblems and were trimmed with officers' pattern koller lace. The oak and laurel wreaths, fringes and tassels were silver. The ornaments and crowns were gold, the latter with silver jewels.

The first panel contained the interlaced initials FAR, the second field showed the Star of the Grand Cross of the House Order of the White Falcon, surrounded by a wreath (half oak and half laurel) and surmounted by a crown. On the eight-pointed silver star was set an eight pointed dark green cross, edged with gold. On a gold medallion in the centre of the cross was a gold ornamented white falcon surrounded by a light blue circle bearing the inscription VIGILANDO ASCENDIMUS.

In the third field were the (modified) Royal Arms of the Kingdom of Saxony, also surrounded by a wreath as above and surmounted by a crown.

The fourth field showed the golden Grand Ducal monogram EW within a wreath as before with a crown over.

The fifth field showed (modified) Great State Arms of the Grand Duchy of Saxe-Weimar-Eisenach, again with the wreath and crown as before.

The sixth field was simply the date December 16, 1905 (date of presentation of the banners by the Colonel-in-Chief of the Regiment, Grand Duke Ernst Wilhelm of Saxe-Weimar-Eisenach) also surrounded by a wreath but in this case the ornamental tracery which ran around the inner edges of the panels was finished off in an intricate design above the date, in lieu of a crown.

4: Prussian Leib-Gendarmerie

THE army gendarmerie were first raised in 1820. Originally there was a detachment allocated to each Army Corps to act as orderlies for the Staff. A 'Garde-Kommando' was reserved for Royal Duties and it was from this small unit that the Leib-Gendarmerie was evolved.

The original uniform of the 'Armee Gendarmerie' was green, faced light blue, with red pipings and yellow metal buttons. On the collar fronts was a single bar of yellow 'Garde-litzen'. The Guard Detachment had the same uniform except that there were two loops of the litzen on the collar fronts. The Royal Gendarmes were now known by the title 'Garde-Reserve-Armee-Kommando' and continued to wear the same uniform except that they now wore large brass stars on the epaulettes.

From 1820 all gendarmes detached for this duty were NCO's and wore the lace and buttons of their rank on the collars and cuffs of their tunics.

In 1824 the detachment received the title 'Leib-Gendarmerie'.

The 'Leib-Gendarmerie' were formed into two troops (Züge). The 1st served the 'Kaiser' and the 2nd carried out orderly duties for the 'Kaiserin'. The Royal Standards were carried by these troops.

UNIFORM AND ACCOUTREMENTS
1 Zug der Leibgendarmerie Sr. Majestät

Helmet: from 1895 a nickel plated, steel cuirassier pattern helmet with a rounded scalloped visor which came to a point in the centre and tombak mountings including the fluted spike. The helmet plate was a German Silver Guard Star with an orange and black enamelled centre. For parades and ceremonial duties when in attendance on the Kaiser the unit wore a tombak crowned eagle in lieu of the helmet spike. This eagle differed in design to that worn by the Gardes du Corps.

Undress Cap: Green with a cornflower blue band and red pipings. The blue band was also piped on either side with red. All gendarmes of the 1st troop, being NCO's, wore small black gutta percha visors on these caps. The Prussian and Reichkokarde were worn in the usual positions on the band and upper part.

Waffenrock: Green with a cornflower blue, red piped collar and cornflower blue cuffs piped with red. The cuffs were pointed. Blue point-ended shoulder straps without piping. Red piping down the front of the coat and on the false pockets and vent in the rear. The collar and the cuffs decorated with yellow 'Garde-litzen' one on each side of collar and one on each cuff. Yellow metal buttons. The shoulder straps decorated with a yellow wool chain-stitched Prussian crown and 'WR II' cypher. Gold NCO lace on the edge of the collar and cuffs. Brass heraldic buttons as appropriate.

Breeches: White melton for ordinary duties and white buckskin for duties in the Palace. The breeches were worn with cuirassier pattern boots. Patent leather for Palace duties.

Long Trousers: Blue/black trousers were worn for walking out. They had red piping down the outside of each leg.

Aiguilettes: White, worked through with black and silver cord and worn on the right shoulder when on duty. The white pouch belt was looped through this aigulette.

Litewka: Universal cavalry pattern with cornflower blue collar patches edged with red piping and blue shoulder straps with the yellow crown and 'WR II' cypher.

Overcoat: Cavalry pattern with cornflower blue collar patches with yellow Garde-litzen and with blue shoulder straps with the yellow crown and cypher. The Gendarmes wore the braid strips of their rank above (and below) the litzen on the collar patches.

RIGHT: The trumpeters of the 1st and 2nd Troops of the Prussian Leib-Gendarmerie. Note the trumpet banners and the method of hooking back the skirts of the waffenrock (Tellgmann).

Schabraque: Dragoon pattern with rounded front and rear. The schrabraque was green with two cornflower blue bands, each of equal widths. The inner edge of the inside blue band and extreme outer edge of the schabraque were piped with red and there was a red band of equal width to the two blue bands, between them.

Trumpeter: Ranked as a Sergeant and wore the heraldic button besides the lace on the collar. Same uniform as the Gendarmes but with the addition of yellow braided blue wings with long woollen fringing. For parade gold laced wings with gold fringing were worn. The sleeves of the tunic were further decorated by vertical gold lace on the front and rear seams and between these three gold chevrons (point down). The trumpet was silver and had a cornflower blue banner with gold crowns in each corner (set on at an angle) and with a large central silver embroidered Guard Star.

Wachtmeister: The 'Erste Wachtmeister' had an additional gold lace strip across the sleeve end of his shoulder strap to distinguish his rank in addition to the extra gold lace band around the sleeve above the cuff (this implies that there was more than one ranking Wachtmeister in the troop for such a distinction to have been necessary). The Erste Wachtmeister carried the lion-headed undress officers' sabre with an officers' sword knot.

Arms: The Gendarmes were armed with the M89 sabre with the Prussian arms set in the basket guard and the M08 pistol for field duties. These were worn on a white leather waistbelt over the coat. The belt had a rectangular brass plate on the front with a white metal Guard Star in its centre.

Standard Bearer: The shield of his appointment (Guard pattern) was worn on the right arm in the authorised manner, and the bandolier was ordered to be the same pattern as the 1st Guard Regiment. However no photograph shows this bandolier being worn, only a plain white pouchbelt.

Officer: The officer of the 1st Troop was detached from a cavalry regiment on a yearly basis. He wore the regimental uniform of his unit plus a handsome gorget.

This ornament had a raised gilt rim and bore on its polished silver centre an ornament comprising a gilt oval plate bearing the ubiquitous Black Eagle surmounted by the Royal Crown and surrounded by a baroque trophy of drums, flags, pikes and muskets.

The chain and the gorget were lined with red velvet. The officer also wore a white lacquered pouch with the Silver Guard Star on its lid and the 1810 pattern lions head sabre.

BELOW: Officers' pattern gorget of the 1st Troop, Prussian Leib-Gendarmerie. RIGHT: Commanding officer of the 1st Troop detached from a Ulan Regiment and wearing his regimental uniform ulanka and wearing the officers' gorget clearly visible on his chest.

2 Zug der Leibgendarmerie der Kaiserin-Potsdam

The second troop was raised on June 28, 1889 especially for orderly service with the Empress. The troopers were drawn from various cuirassier regiments and the NCO's from the Leib Kürassier Regiment No 1. The unit was commanded by an officer from the Kürassier Regiment Königin. The gendarmes of this troop did not therefore all rank as NCO's.

UNIFORM AND ACCOUTREMENTS

Helmet: As the 1st troop.

Undress Cap: White with a carmine red band and piping and with the two normal cockades. As gendarmes did not all rank as NCO's only the latter wore the small black visor.

Waffenrock: White kirsey with carmine red collar, pointed cuffs and skirt linings (these latter could be hooked up when on horseback to show the carmine inside). Crimson piping down the front and on the back vent and false pocket flaps. Shoulder straps white piped carmine but without any device. Gardelitzen and buttons white, the former with a carmine central 'light'. Two loops of lace on each collar front and one on each cuff. NCO's lace was silver. The aigulette was worn on this coat as for the 1st troop.

Blue Waffenrock: This very dark blue coat was worn by the 2nd troop for undress duties. It had the same distinctions as the white coat, and was worn with black trousers with carmine stripes for walking out.

Housings and Wallets: Cuirassier pattern, carmine red with white bands and piping. The wallets and the rear corners of the housing decorated with white Guard Star and yellow crowns. Set on at an angle on the latter.

Trumpeter: Carmine wings with white braid and fringes, silver for parades. A carmine red trumpet banner with silver Guard Star and yellow crowns and silver fringe.

Arms: As for the 1st troop.

Officer: From 1895 the Officer of the 2nd Troop wore the gorget of the Kürassier Regiment No 2.

CASTLE FESTIVE DRESS

For duties with the Empress within the Palace the 2nd Troop wore a special uniform known as the Schloss-Galabekleidung (Castle Festive Dress).

The uniform was in the old 18th century Prussian style with a white kirsey coat with a stand and fall collar which was carmine red on the outside. The coat had narrow carmine lapels to the waist decorated with three pairs of white tasselled loops on each (black and white for the NCO's). The garment had carmine red turnbacks and the pockets were also piped carmine. Under the coat was a single-breasted white waistcoat with eight silver buttons down the front and three on each pocket. White breeches and patent leather cuirassier boots completed the lower part of the costume. The head-dress comprised a black felt cocked hat with a silver cord and button and a black and silver old style Prussian cockade. The standing hair plume was white with a black base. The old pattern Prussian sabre was carried in a brown leather scabbard. The sword knot was white for the gendarmes and with the expected black and white crown for the NCO's. The Wachtmeister wore the silver and black old Prussian Portepee. Short white gloves were worn by NCO's and gendarmes.

The Officer of the 2nd Troop also wore this costume but with silver scalloped lace and a silver chain loop on the hat. The feather was white over black. The coat was in finer material than that worn by the other ranks and had a special silver lace on the lapels and the cuffs, this was in the form of a daisy flower, close petalled with a curved stalk ending in a loose tassel. The old Prussian silk sash was tied on the left side and worn under the coat but over the waistcoat. The officer wore cuffed gloves.

All ranks wore the aigulette on the right shoulder, the officers' silver pattern had the cypher 'WR II' in gilt on the shoulder part.

LEIBGENDARMERIE STANDARDS

The 1st Troop carried the 'Kaiserstandarte': A rectangular golden yellow standard having as its main ornament a large black Iron Cross which stretched from edge to edge. Superimposed over the cross the shield of the House of Hohenzollern bearing in its centre the Black Eagle of Hohenzollern. On the breast of this eagle another shield bearing another black eagle, in this case crowned and carrying the orb and sceptre and with a black and white quartered shield on its breast. The larger eagle has a red tongue, beak and talons, the smaller eagle golden crown, beak, talons, orb and sceptre. Encircling the larger shield the collar of the Black Eagle.

The collar was alternately black and gold heraldic eagles and a gold edged, light blue circlet enclosing an intricate FR monogram in gold edged light green letters. In the centre of these was a gold edged white disc bearing the inscription SUUM CUIQUE, also in gold. Set around the perimeter of the circlet were four gold crowns.

On the large shield the Kaiser's crown in gold silver and red. The four arms of the Iron Cross lettered 'GOTT' (top) 'MIT' (left) 'UNS' (right) and 1870 (bottom) in white. The cross trimmed with an inner border of white set slightly in from the edge. Each corner of the flag (within the arms of the cross) decorated with three black eagles and a large gold, silver and red crown. The staff was black and topped with a silver spike.

The 2nd Troop carried the 'Kaiserinstandarte': A similar shaped standard in golden yellow cloth but without the massive Iron Cross. In the centre a shield decorated with eagles as for the Kaiser's Standard. The shield encircled by the collar of the Order of the Black Eagle and topped by the Kaiserin's crown. The field of the standard covered by black eagles and with an Iron Cross in the top left canton, in its centre a white 'W' and '1870' at the bottom of the lower arm.

BOOKS FOR FUTURE READING

Freiherr von Zedlitz-Neukirch —	Geschichte des Kgl. Preuss. Leib-Kürassier-Regiment 'Grosser Kurfürst' (Schlesisches) No 1. Volume III.
C. Kling —	Gesichte der Bekleidung, Bewaffnung und Austrüstung des Kgl. Preuss. Heeres. Volume II.
Krickel-Lange —	Das Deutsche Reichsheer in seiner neusten Bekleidung und Ausrüstung.
A. Mila —	Uniformirungs-liste des Deutsche Heeres.
H. Knötel Baron Collas E. Janke	Friedensuniformen das deutsche heer bei Ausbruch des Weltkrieges.
H. Jurgens —	Uniformen des Deutschen Heeres im Juli 1914.
F. Schirmer F. Wiener	Die Kürassier und Schweren Reiter Regimenter der Alten Armee.
Col. R. H. Rankin	Helmets and Headdresses of the Imperial German Army 1870-1918.